Student Diversity

Teaching strategies to meet the learning needs
of all students in K-10 classrooms

FAYE BROWNLIE

CATHERINE FENIAK

LEYTON SCHNELLERT

3rd Edition

Pembroke Publishers Limited

To all of the teachers that we have had the privilege to work beside
and to the many amazing students who have taught us
to be stronger teachers

© 2016 Pembroke Publishers
538 Hood Road
Markham, Ontario, Canada L3R 3K9
www.pembrokepublishers.com

Distributed in the U.S. by Stenhouse Publishers
480 Congress Street
Portland, ME 04101
www.stenhouse.com

Funded by the Government of Canada
Financé par le gouvernement du Canada | **Canada** Ontario
Ontario Media Development
Corporation
Société de développement
de l'industrie des médias
de l'Ontario

Library and Archives Canada Cataloguing in Publication

Brownlie, Faye, author
    Student diversity : teaching strategies to meet the learning needs of all students in
K-10 Classrooms / Faye Brownlie, Catherine Feniak, Leyton Schnellert. -- 3rd edition.

Includes bibliographical references and index.
Issued in print and electronic formats.
ISBN 978-1-55138-318-7 (paperback).--ISBN 978-1-55138-920-2 (pdf)

    1. Inclusive education--Canada. 2. Mixed ability grouping in education--Canada.
I. Feniak, Catherine, author II. Schnellert, Leyton, author III. Title.

LC1200.B76 2016   371.9'0460971   C2016-904203-0
                                            C2016-904204-9

Editor: Kate Revington
Cover Design: John Zehethofer
Typesetting: Jay Tee Graphics Ltd.

Printed and bound in Canada
9 8 7 6 5 4 3 2

FSC
www.fsc.org
MIX
Paper from
responsible sources
FSC® C004071

Contents

Preface

It is hard to believe that 10 years have passed since the second edition of *Student Diversity*. So much has happened, yet so much remains the same. We continue to be passionate about inclusion: the right of all students to belong and to learn with their peers in the regular classroom as much as possible and the responsibility of all educators to collaboratively build learning environments that make this possible.

With this is mind, we have woven examples from the primary and early years into this edition of *Student Diversity*. Thanks go to Lisa Schwartz, Cindy Lee, Terra McKenzie, Belinda Chi, Don Blazevich, Ray Appel, Sarbjit Sidhu, Stacey Shaw, Jackie Hawthorn, and Kristan Thompson for welcoming us into their learning spaces and sharing their wisdom with us.

Research continues to support the idea that teachers' collaboration and professionalism can have a powerful impact on students' lives. Our tasks as leaders of learning are too important and too complex for us to work alone. Together, we are better, and we *need* to be better. Canada continues to welcome immigrants from around the world. We have more refugee children than ever before. We have students with special needs that are new to us and that challenge us to learn with the students. As school psychologists and media reports confirm, we have more anxious learners. We have changing curricula requiring teachers to be more professional, more knowledgeable about big ideas and learning theory, more connected to parents, and more transparent in our assessment. The expectations are huge; the rewards of teaching, endless; the joy of learning, priceless.

In the 2007 McKinsey report, *How the World's Best-Performing School Systems Come Out on Top*, it was reported that top-performing systems recognize that the only way to improve outcomes is to improve instruction: learning occurs when students and teachers interact, and thus, to improve learning implies improving the quality of that interaction. Canada is a top-performing system. We continue to focus on the power of the interaction, the quality of the teaching in our classrooms. We continue to reflect, alone and together, on what makes a difference in learning for *all* of our students. What worked today? What can we do differently tomorrow?

In 2010, another McKinsey report on education, *How the World's Most Improved School Systems Keep Getting Better*, was issued. The follow-up report to the 2007 publication explained that systems that continued to improve focused on collaborative practice and that collaborative practice resulted in shared responsibility for all learners, shifting the focus from what teachers teach to what students learn, and teachers becoming custodians of a shared model of "good instruction."

We three teachers continue to work towards schools and classrooms where we share responsibility for all learners, where we teach responsively, attending closely to the impact that our teaching is having on our learners, where we share a model of "good instruction" and work to implement it minute by minute, day by day. Achieving this degree of professionalism is a challenge and a responsibility that we embrace.

Aren't we fortunate to be together learning, doing our part to build an inclusive society that recognizes and values diversity? Aren't we *all* fortunate to have opportunities to improve the quality of our instruction for the benefit of our students?

Faye Brownlie
Catherine Feniak
Leyton Schnellert

Introduction: Improving Learning for All

The headlines in our weekend newspaper screamed **"Who are we calling Special?"** In the lead article, the president of British Columbia's Middle Years Provincial Intermediate Teachers' Association (myPITA), Ray Myrtle, was quoted as saying, *"We don't have the tools; we don't have the time"* to address the learning needs of all the students in the class. That was 29 October 2005 in *The Vancouver Sun*.

Comments like that have propelled us to put our ideas on paper, to write the first, the second, and now the third edition of *Student Diversity*. We believe it is time — still time — to work differently in our schools, in order to better meet the needs of a diverse group of students. We believe that tools do exist for teaching all students, but that they may not be the tools we have used traditionally. We believe that teachers need to share the contents of their respective toolboxes and how they use their tools successfully, alone and together.

Towards a Model of Collaboration

In the past, as resource teachers, we worked with select groups of students to assess their learning, to teach them specific skills, to catch them up, to teach them differently, to give them more individual attention and time. In this role, we were very much captains of our own ships, running programs and occasionally consulting with teachers as to how they could best support our students when they were in the other teachers' classrooms. We often saw significant progress with our students, particularly when they were in a supported learning situation, in other words, learning with us in a small group. Unfortunately, we also heard this comment: "He may do that with you, but in the classroom with everyone else . . ." We often wished we could have more time with these students in order to really make a difference.

Then, also as resource teachers, we came to work more collaboratively with classroom teachers. In this model, each of us focuses time and effort on supporting the classroom teacher and the diverse class, including all students. Learning resource teacher and classroom teacher work together, pooling expertise and resources. We assess the students using provincial performance standards to see what they can do and what they need to be able to do. We use this assessment to design lessons and units that move the students towards accomplishing curriculum goals. In the role of resource teacher, we sometimes work side by side with the classroom teacher, in the classroom, focusing on how best to support the learning of all students in the context of the ongoing learning expectations. We find that our collaboration increases learning time for students and increases everyone's skill set: our toolbox.

As classroom teachers, we know the weight of responsibility of trying to teach classrooms of diverse students, sometimes feeling that it is just too much, that what we have always done is no longer working. But we also know that there are classrooms where learning *is* happening for all students. We know that books, workshops, and online presentations are available to take us beyond the confines of our personal experiences. We know that when we work as a team in a school we *can* make a difference to student learning, we *can* improve our competencies, and we *can* leave at the end of the day, confident not only that our students feel as though they belong in our class but that they — and we — have evidence that they are progressing along their respective learning journeys.

Building Vibrant Learning Environments

Current brain research and learning theory support what intuitive teachers have long known:

- Students need to be actively engaged in learning.
- Students need to belong to a strong community in the classroom.
- Students need to see themselves as able and capable, self-regulating learners.
- Students need to set personal learning goals.
- Students need to learn in a variety of ways.
- Students need to be emotionally involved in their learning.
- Students need rich, in-depth inquiry.
- Students learn at different rates.
- Students learn best when the content is connected to the world and to their lives.
- Students need choice and clear expectations.

These are foundation statements for our classrooms, and you will see evidence of them in the scenarios presented in this resource. This book is meant to provide teachers with new tools to enable them to better support all the students in their classes, and with ideas on how to minimize their planning time and increase the learning time for their students.

Some scenarios described here in *Student Diversity*, third edition, are situated in single-grade classrooms, Kindergarten to Grade 7, but most are situated in combined or multi-age classrooms from Kindergarten to Grade 7, and single-grade classrooms from Grades 8 to 10. New in this third edition is the inclusion of primary and early years lessons. All the classes support full inclusion of learners with special needs and a collaborative learning resource model. Each has been affected by a large influx of learners who are learning English as a second or third language. Teachers in these classes are trying to make sense of a curriculum organized by grade-mandated learning outcomes or expectations, criterion-referenced assessment, provincial performance standards, and current learning theory.

Strategies Vital to Student Learning

In *Reading Next: A Vision for Action and Research in Middle and High School Literacy*, authors Gina Biancarosa and Catherine Snow present an interesting mathematical equation:

$$15 - 3 = 0.$$

They suggest that there are 15 research-based strategies to improve adolescent literacy.

Two resources that contain more detail on the 15 research-based strategies are *It's All about Thinking: Collaborating to Support All Learners in English, Social Studies, and Humanities* by Faye Brownlie and Leyton Schnellert and *It's All about Thinking: Collaborating to Support All Learners in Mathematics and Science* by Faye Brownlie, Carole Fullerton, and Leyton Schnellert.

The 15 Strategies to Improve Literacy	
1. Direct, explicit comprehension instruction	9. Ongoing formative assessment of students
2. Effective instructional principles embedded in content	10. Extended time for literacy
3. Motivation and self-directed learning	11. Professional development
4. Text-based collaborative learning	12. Ongoing summative assessment of students and programs
5. Strategic tutoring	13. Teacher teams
6. Diverse texts	14. Leadership
7. Intensive writing	15. A comprehensive and coordinated literacy program
8. A technology component	

They also suggest that none of these strategies will make a difference to student learning unless teachers incorporate the three vital strategies identified below:

1. **Professional Development:** Teachers cannot improve student literacy alone. The needs are constantly changing. The knowns are constantly growing. We must provide structures to support the learning of all our teachers.

2. **Ongoing Formative Assessment of Students:** To make the greatest difference, we must use our assessment information to inform our instruction.

3. **Ongoing Summative Assessment of Students and Programs:** We are responsible for checking and seeing that what we are doing is making a positive difference.

It is our hope that *Student Diversity*, third edition, contributes to this discussion. We present to you the best of what we have learned from collaborations with teachers who are using their time and tools to make a difference to the learning of all their students. You may be in a teaching situation without the benefit of a team or a professional learning community. Perhaps *Student Diversity*, third edition, will become part of your team. Join us as we endeavour to put into practice the best of what we know. Together, we can improve learning for all.

1 The Classroom as a Learning Community

Imagine a combined Grades 4 and 5 class of 29 students. Of this 29, four are level-one and level-two (just beginning) students for whom English is an additional language. Five are identified as level-three ELL (English Language Learner); one is diagnosed as having a severe behavior disorder and is on medication to assist him in self-control and in monitoring his behavior; one is extremely challenged to control his behavior but has not been identified as having special needs; and one student has a learning disability in the area of expressive output. Support is available for these students, largely on a pull-out basis, from the ELL teacher, the resource teacher for students with severe learning disabilities, and the area counsellor. Another student in the class sees the area counsellor weekly in a friendship group. Added to this, the learning-assistance teacher supports students who require short-term intervention.

Each of the professionals who support these "children with special needs" is capable and highly supportive of the students and of the classroom teacher. The end result in the classroom, however, is a constantly revolving door. The teacher is left wondering what is actually happening with all the programming for these students, and what she can do to support their learning in her classroom, where they spend most of their time. Some days, the whole class is together in the classroom for no more than 30 minutes. This situation has made it challenging to build a classroom community where students respect one another and value diversity.

The Centrality of the Classroom Teacher

Return to the same school two years later. Many of these students are now in a combined Grades 6 and 7 class. The class composition is similar, but the school has shifted to a collaborative, non-categorical support model. In this model, the classroom teacher is central and is involved in the design of how support services will be provided to her students. One learning resource teacher is assigned to each class, and together the classroom teacher and learning resource teacher establish a plan of how best to address the learning of all the students in the class, including those identified with special needs. The time available for the learning resource teacher to work with the classroom teacher is equal to the combined times of the former various support teachers.

Each team — resource teacher and classroom teacher — receives two hours of planning time at the beginning of the year to determine their course of action. After that, if more planning time is required, it is sought out on an "as needed" basis. Some students, especially level-one ELL students, may be pulled out of the classroom for direct instruction from time to time as needed.

However, most of the support occurs *in* the classroom, where both teachers work with all of the students on their agreed-upon plan. In this classroom, all students learn together for most of the day.

The Rationale for Inclusion

Inclusion — enrolling all students in age-appropriate, regular classrooms — is the norm in North America. It is based on the following beliefs:

- Students belong in the regular classroom.
- Students learn best when they are valued members of a community.
- Deep learning and skill development happen in context.
- Students with special needs require ongoing effective programming.
- This programming is best provided when a classroom teacher and a single resource teacher collaborate to better meet diverse needs.

In a non-categorical model, one learning resource teacher for the class works with the classroom teacher to address the needs of all students.

Inclusion affects all teachers, not just the regular classroom teacher. When we speak of a "non-categorical model of resource support," we mean that the one learning resource teacher for the class works with the classroom teacher to address the needs of all students: students who are learning English as an additional language, the severely learning challenged, the intellectually challenged, students with severe behavior disorders, the physically and multiply challenged, the culturally diverse, students who have mild to moderate learning disabilities or communication disorders, students who are gifted learners.

Moving from Fragmentation to Communities of Learners

The traditional support model often resulted in fragmentation of the classroom, as students came and went to see specialist teachers.

In the past, the support model was based on aligning specific students with specific support teachers. This practice often resulted in fragmentation of the classroom, as students came and went to see specialist teachers. These specialist teachers searched for time to collaborate with classroom teachers to plan for and reinforce the students' specific learning goals when these students were in the regular classroom. Working in a collaborative, non-categorical resource model does not preclude one-on-one time outside the classroom for specific students, nor occasional pull-out programs. The main focus, however, is providing more effective programming for all students for as much time as possible each day.

We are trying to create a community within the classroom to support learning. All students, including students identified as having special needs, are the responsibility of the classroom teacher. It is critical that we reduce the number of contacts the classroom teacher has with people whose job is to support the learning of identified students. Too much fragmentation does not support maintaining a vibrant, cohesive learning community.

The Non-categorical Model

In Elementary School

In our preferred model of support — non-categorical — the roles of the support teachers are amalgamated into a resource support team. A classroom teacher is assigned one non-categorical resource person for a number of periods per week, based on need. The learning resource teacher works with several classroom teachers, but not the entire school staff (or typically not the entire staff during the same term or chunk of time in a school with just one learning resource teacher). Together, the two teachers work out a plan to support the learning of all the students in the classroom, including those identified with special needs. The support provided by the learning resource teacher can occur either inside or outside the classroom, but the plan for support is a collaboration of the two professionals, and is curriculum based. Appropriate accommodations for learners (formerly referred to as "adaptations and modifications") are tied to learners' needs and to grade-level expectations or learning outcomes.

The spillover from non-categorical support affects many more students than in the traditional support model. Among the students who benefit are those who are not identified for an individual education plan (IEP), but who need additional teacher time and expertise.

The learning resource teachers meet as a team weekly to consult with one another. This team may include an ELL teacher, a teacher of the learning disabled, a learning-assistance teacher, and a teacher with a specialty in autism or behavior disorders. However, in their daily work, they assist all students. In their weekly meetings, they share their expertise and help one another solve the ongoing challenges of the classes in which they work. Bringing one's special skills to the table enhances the capacity of all involved. The learning resource teachers are the link to outside support teams (e.g., speech and language clinicians, school psychologists, counsellors, and district-level special education consultants), leaving the classroom teacher freer to concentrate on designing effective learning sequences within the classroom.

In Middle School

The developmental uniqueness of students in this age group lends itself to students working with fewer teachers than they will experience in secondary school. Teachers plan in teams to develop ideas and approaches, and a learning resource teacher works with one or two of these teams. Together, classroom and support teachers create classroom learning experiences for students that offer more pathways to learning; engage them in making connections among themselves, the world, and big ideas; and develop all students' competencies within the regular classroom. When learning resource teachers work with classroom teachers with a focus on all students' learning, planning can be proactive. Together, classroom and support teachers carry out and use formative assessment information to co-plan and co-teach, and what is most important, to build in supports for diverse learners right from the beginning. Where possible, the school timetable is designed to allow team planning time, with the learning resource teacher there as part of the team.

In Secondary School

In secondary schools, the benefits of decreasing the number of support teachers involved with students and teachers are many. In secondary school, students and teachers often struggle to see the whole picture: classes are taught by several different teachers, and students do not realize that they can or should use the same effective learning strategies in multiple settings.

Many schools have had significant success when a single learning resource teacher aligns with a single grade and a cross-curricular team of teachers. When a team chooses key strategies and skills to target across a grade, the learning resource teacher can assist them in modeling these strategies, adapting them

The key to matching teaching strategies to outcomes is remembering that a strategy is *most* effective when it supports the specific, required learning. Sometimes students use a strategy because of its familiarity and that choice of strategy might not be effective in that particular learning context.

across subject areas; this teacher can also assist the team in making units of study more accessible for all students. By introducing supports that address an individual student's learning needs, but can be used by all students — for example, text sets, visual supports, highlighting of key routines, and specific teaching strategies — many more students benefit. Often, learning resource teachers co-teach in the classrooms, helping to introduce and reinforce key strategies, supports, and routines from class to class. Everyone in the school community benefits when the learning resource teacher is seen as a valuable and integral member of the team.

Many secondary resource teachers who embrace this model have shared how classroom teachers better understand the many aspects of their work and how they have built stronger relationships with colleagues. All the students who receive support benefit through access to the core curriculum in the context of the regular classroom. They are given an opportunity to experience success the first time they encounter the content, instead of waiting for a chance to be retaught in the resource room. Everyone in the classroom has a better opportunity to see and experience previously recommended accommodations in action.

How This Model of Support Affects Participants

When a school implements the collaborative, non-categorical model, all participants, including classroom teacher, students, and parents, benefit from the approach. This change in service delivery model affects each participant differently.

Classroom Teacher

- Less time is needed to meet with support teachers to plan for, coordinate, and reinforce programming for students with special needs. Because both teachers are together in the room, the question "What did you do with my kids today?" is self-evident.
- With collaborative planning, accommodations to enable students with special needs to access the ongoing program in the classroom is easier.
- Building a classroom community where all students belong and learn together is possible.
- The expertise of the learning resource teacher is more available for the classroom teacher and her learning.
- Delivery of the curriculum becomes more differentiated.
- The learning resource teacher and the classroom teacher provide each other with a second set of eyes. Both teachers gain feedback on the effectiveness of their instruction and where student learning breaks down.
- Support is instantaneous for more students when the second teacher is in the classroom.
- The saying "Two heads are better than one" holds true. The collaboration not only provides more direct service to students, but the emphasis on sharing and the opportunity for sharing expertise are central. This is a professional learning community in action.
- All members of the classroom have a better idea of the purpose of classroom activities and their goal.

Learning Resource Teacher

- The non-categorical model needs only a short startup time. Direct service to students can begin almost immediately, instead of having inordinate amounts of time spent in time-tabling, assessment, individualized (separate) planning, and trying to consult and collaborate with teachers after class.
- Rather than teaching concepts or skills separate from the curriculum, the learning resource teacher has the opportunity to work alongside an experienced curriculum specialist to co-plan how best to integrate the competency development into learning sequences and adapt expectations for the learners with special needs.
- The specialized programming that used to occur in the resource room, which needed reinforcement in the classroom to really benefit the student, is now easier because both teachers can observe each other work and together support the learning of students.
- The learning resource teacher gains an understanding of the curriculum expectations of the students and can use his/her expertise to support students' developing skills, rather than working with a remedial model of learning.
- Weekly resource team meetings provide a trusting environment for asking questions and sharing expertise.
- The focus is on service delivery. There is a shift from concern with labeling to increased concern with addressing the learning needs of students.
- There are fewer classroom teachers to consult with, and the consultation is less on "what we did and what you need to do" and more on "what we can do together."
- The expertise and skill of the learning resource teacher is not reserved for labeled students; most students can benefit from more extensive strategic repertoires.

Students

- Programming for the students who are most at-risk in learning is more consistent.
- Accommodations to enable access to the curriculum are the focus.
- Support is seamless, so intermediate and middle-years students need not suffer the indignity of being removed from their peer group for extra help.
- Feedback on performance towards the learning outcomes of the curriculum is faster. Student performance improves with appropriate, immediate feedback, followed by a chance to practise, both with a coach and independently.
- Identifying students in need of support is a less arduous task. With two teachers present at key times, a formalized referral process becomes almost nonexistent and the focus is immediately on student need. The key question: *Who needs what support in order to be able to access the learning?* Students do not need to wait to be tested for identification before receiving service.
- Students have access to learning supports developed for and introduced in their classrooms.

Parents

- There are no mixed messages. The learning resource teacher and the classroom teacher align their goals for the student when engaged in continuous, ongoing, side-by-side teaching.
- There are fewer people to talk to after reporting and in IEP (individual education plan) meetings. Less intimidation for the family follows from fewer required meetings of the full team with the family.
- The classroom teacher — or possibly the support teacher — will become the primary contact for the parent. This keeps the system from overwhelming the parent with contacts.
- Student learning is enhanced.
- Their children will not only attend a regular school and a regular class, but will belong in it.

A Comment on Our Examples of Support Delivery

Further information about how to establish a non-categorical resource team in your school is presented in *Learning in Safe Schools*, second edition, by Faye Brownlie and Judith King.

The teaching experiences outlined in this book have occurred in schools that embrace the non-categorical model of support delivery. You will notice as you read that there are times when two teachers are working together in the class and other times when the classroom teacher is alone with the students. Most of the service to students with special needs is delivered within the classroom.

Rarely are students removed from the class for support. When they are removed, however, the learning expectations and the program have been co-planned by the teacher and the learning resource teacher, and the alternative setting has been deemed to be more beneficial to the student's learning.

First Week Considerations

During the first week with a new class, we set the tone for the year. We involve the students in a variety of structured activities that require them to meet others in the room, engage in discussion, share their findings when reporting back to class, reflect on their learning and on their participation, share their interests, passions, and background knowledge, ask questions, process new information in different ways, and experience learning as an opportunity for connecting, processing, and transforming and personalizing new information (see pages 21 to 24).

The classroom is meant to be a community where all students belong. It must be a safe place for everyone.

One of the few classroom rules that we officially establish with the students is that the classroom must be a safe place for everyone. Students will not take risks in sharing their ideas and fully participating in activities if they perceive that others criticize their opinions. They also will not want to engage in group activities if they feel that they are not welcome to join a particular group. It is critical for the classroom to become a community where all students belong.

Establishing Working Groups

During the first or second class, the students in intermediate, middle, and secondary classes are placed in working groups. This can be done randomly or by taking into account the students' requests. Students in primary classes work with partners, changing frequently.

Initially, the students are placed into working groups. If many students in the class know each other already, we work with a quick sociogram based on their writing down the names of two classmates with whom they would like to work. At a glance we can see which names appear frequently, which not at all, what patterns or cliques are apparent. The goal in forming groups is to support and include all learners. Using these lists we try to work in some of the requests each time we make class groupings. Students are guaranteed that, at some point in the year, they will get their first and second choices of group mates.

Much useful information is gained from this sociogram:

- We notice which students are willing to work with any members of the class. These are often students who may be empathetic to all students, including those with special educational needs. We do not want empathetic students exclusively in groups with students with special needs (or vice versa), but at the beginning of the year they can, with only a little support and coaching, be peer models of inclusion for the rest of the class.
- We take note of which students are most and least frequently listed in the student requests. Many times students want the opportunity to work with another student who is not usually in their social group but who is perceived to be academically strong. Students who look beyond their immediate social group for working partners may be ones we want to enlist as peer models in the development of social skills.
- The students whose names appear infrequently are carefully placed in groups. Before beginning group work, the class talks about the look and sound of a group that is working productively. We circulate throughout the class during group work, assisting students in including all members of the group, in finding cooperative ways of speaking to each other, and in resolving conflict.

We truly believe in the social aspect of learning and in the students' strong desire to belong. Our personal goal for group work is that, by the end of the year, each student in the class can work with any other student in the class, in a way that promotes the learning of all members of the group.

Day 1: A People Search

Participating in this People Search on the first day alerts the students to the fact that they are in a class where talking is expected. As we listen to the noise and notice their smiles, we are reminded of what on-task, engaged, happy students look like and sound like. We hope to keep this in mind throughout the year.

Having students make lists of preferred group mates, of course, does not work if most of the students are new to one other because, for example, they are entering a large middle or secondary school from a variety of elementary feeder schools. If this is the case, we proceed to a People Search to help students learn their classmates' names and begin to become acquainted.

During the first week, we want activities that will require students to move about the room and speak to one another. In a People Search, students must ask their classmates a series of questions in order to discover some of the things that were done over the summer holiday (see the People Search line master, page 20). In this way, every member of the class is approached by others and every member must initiate some conversations. The students love finding out about each other's summers. Even the students who are learning English as a second or third language actively participate. Once they have heard a question asked, students can use this as a model for approaching others. We move among the students, bridging as necessary to ensure that all are included.

People Search

Have each person sign in only once. Find someone who, over the summer . . .

• played a lot of online games _____ _____ _____ Signature	• made a new friend _____ _____ _____ Signature
• traveled by train or by boat _____ _____ _____ Signature	• learned how to do something new _____ _____ _____ Signature
• enjoyed spending time alone _____ _____ _____ Signature	• read a great book _____ _____ _____ Signature
• went somewhere they had never been before _____ _____ _____ Signature	• camped _____ _____ _____ Signature

Pembroke Publishers © 2016 *Student Diversity*, 3rd ed., by Faye Brownlie, Catherine Feniak, Leyton Schnellert ISBN 978-1-55138-318-7

Days 2 and 3: A Strategic Sequence

Having now established working groups, we are ready to begin a lesson sequence with a piece of text. There are many different sequences from which to choose. The sequences are built from strategies, each strategy chosen to match a particular purpose:

- **connecting** with background knowledge and with others, building personal questions
- **processing** new information by interacting with it, making new connections, revising former understandings
- **transforming and personalizing** new information so it is stored in long-term memory

We present two different sequences. Both have a low floor and a high ceiling; in other words, the strategies are open-ended enough that all can participate and they also give room for students to be creative. Both model the active learning we expect in the classroom.

Sequence 1: Questioning — Quadrants of a Thought — Information Write

Choose a non-fiction picture book. One book we have used is the picture book *A River Ran Wild* by Lynne Cherry, about a river endangered by pollution.

Sequence 1 consists of these strategies:
1. Questioning (connecting)
2. Quadrants of a Thought (processing)
3. Information Write (transforming and personalizing)

1. Questioning

- Choose three pictures from the text to share with the students.
- Place the students in groups of four.
- Ask this question of each group: "What do you wonder when you look at this picture?" Have them record their questions. Encourage students to wonder, but to resist the urge to answer each other's questions.
- Repeat the above process with the two other pictures, changing the recorder in each group with each picture.
- Ask students to choose their most creative question to share from the first picture, their most thoughtful from the second, and their most imaginative in the third.
- Collect and share these questions from the groups. Try to talk about the questions without answering them. Doing this allows the students to search for personal answers before reading and as they hear the text.
- Discuss the process used in each group to come to a consensus on which question to choose. Doing this gives you more information on what social skills to emphasize in the coming weeks.

2. Quadrants of a Thought

It is often helpful to have students initially concentrate on two boxes during the reading and add ideas to the others during the class discussion at each break in the reading.

- Have each student fold a piece of paper into four and label the boxes Images, Words, Senses, and Emotions.
- Ask students to collect ideas in at least two of the quadrants as you read.
- Read the text to the students, stopping three times for class discussion, in which students can share what they are including in their quadrants.

- As the students share their written and pictorial ideas with each other, encourage them to look for parallels and differences in their thinking.

3. Information Write

- Have a class discussion focusing on what was learned, discovering what surprised the students, and if using *A River Ran Wild*, comparing the event in the book to the state of local rivers. (This sequence is based on the idea that you have been saving newspaper clippings on pollution in local rivers or other local environmental issues on which people are taking a stand.)
- Students write an information paragraph about what they have learned from the text, from the discussion, and from local news stories.

Primary students are better supported in focusing on fewer strategies at this time. *A Salmon for Simon* by Betty Waterton is one of our preferred texts. Begin with "questioning," but keep the students together as a class and keep this as an oral activity. Encourage each student to ask a question for the first picture, then the second, then the third. Students can now write what they anticipate the text will be about before listening to the reading of the text. Then, after the reading, they can discuss how the author surprised them and extended their thinking, as well as how their thinking matched that of the author.

Sequence 2: Think-Aloud — Visual Thinking — Found Poem

Choose a text. We often use the *Salmon Creek* by Annette LeBox and Karen Reczuch, about the life cycle of the Pacific salmon.

Sequence 2 consists of these strategies:
1. Think-Aloud (connecting)
2. Visual Thinking (processing)
3. Found Poem (transforming and personalizing)

1. Think-Aloud

- Write the first few lines of the text on the Smart Board for all to see. *Salmon Creek* opens with this:

> THESE were Sumi's first memories:
> water over stones,
> the scent of creek,
> darkness so complete
> she could barely imagine
> another world larger
> than the egg case enclosing her.

- Read this to the students, explaining what is going on in your mind as you read. For example, you might read, "These were Sumi's first memories:" and then say:

> I wonder who Sumi is? I think this sounds like a girl's name and I guess she owns the memories because of the apostrophe. This makes me wonder about how you can tell a "first" memory. I don't think mine are from when I was really young. I notice this line ends with a colon. That usually means a list is coming. I predict the list will be a list of her memories.

- Continue thinking aloud as you read.
- Brainstorm with the students to identify the strategies you used in reading. Record them where the class can see the names.

- Write the next piece of text on the Smart Board. Choose a short piece, as you did with the first excerpt.
- Place the students in partners. One student will read the piece of text aloud to the other, thinking aloud to show the connections, questions, and ideas he/she has while reading. The second partner will coach. The students may choose to use any of the strategies you used, or they may use others.
- Add to the brainstormed list other strategies the students identify.
- The partner who was initially the coach now does the think-aloud while the other partner coaches. Again, after the discussion, add to the brainstormed strategy list.
- Compliment the students on the depth and breadth of the reading strategies they have identified. Reinforce that this active reading is what creates long-term memory and what engages readers with text.

2. Visual Thinking

- Have the students draw a large thinking bubble on their papers.
- Continue to read the text aloud, not showing the pictures. Have the students draw the images they have in their minds as you read.
- After reading a few pages, stop and collect some of the images that the students are recording.
- Remind the students that ideas are meant to be shared in this class and that it is a compliment if someone borrows one of their ideas.
- Continue reading and collecting images for several pages.
- Have the students review their images and try to label them with specific language they have heard in the text. It is helpful to model this labeling. Students may wish to label with a partner. The labeling helps them synthesize their thinking about the text, and recall and build specific text language.
- Finish reading the text by just reading.

3. Found Poem

- Reread the text the next day, showing the illustrations.
- Read the first quarter of the text again. As you read, have the students focus on words or phrases that are so significant that they stay ringing in their ears, even after the text has been read.
- Stop at the end of the first quarter and ask those students whose birthdays are in three months you identify (one quarter of the year) to stand. Each of these students will contribute a word or phrase. Together, the students will build a poem that captures the essence of this part of the text. Because they are creating poetry, repetitions are fine, and phrase or sentence length may vary from one word to many. Students are always amazed at how poetic they sound and at the many ways these phrases can be ordered to create a different sounding poem.
- Repeat this process, stopping after another quarter of the poem and having students whose birthdays are in a different set of three months make a poem.
- Continue until all the text has been read and all students have contributed to a found poem. Talk with the students about flow and connections, and about the ease with which they have collaboratively constructed a poem.

- Now, students, alone or in partners, write a found poem based on their interpretation of the text, their response to the text, a retelling of the text, or whatever you choose the focus for writing to be.

Primary students enjoy the play of language of creating an oral found poem from books that are read aloud. They listen for words or phrases that they want to remember and share them in short poems (organized by shoes with/without Velcro, those with laces, those with toes we can see, . . .). Sometimes we read the text twice to the students before beginning to create the poem. Our younger students have enjoyed creating found poems from *A Dog Is a Dog* by Stephen Shaskan and *Stellaluna* by Janell Cannon.

Middle and secondary learners also benefit greatly from these kinds of sequences. There are terrific resources related to environmental and social issues that lend themselves to such sequences. *Weslandia* by Paul Fleischman is a hit in middle school, and *Tales from Outer Suburbia* by Shaun Tan, a hit in secondary school. Working together in this way creates community and sets a classroom tone that encourages collaboration, the communication of diverse perspectives, and critical and creative thinking.

Week 1 in Review

All of our students are better able to participate if we allow them talk time, some movement, repetition, small-group work, and opportunities to draw and write to express their thinking before requiring a written response.

These initial strategies have been deliberately chosen because they do not require participation solely through print or relying only on individual response. They allow students with special needs to participate and help those learning English to acquire the language of the curriculum while they are developing their ability to use the English language. The specific activities have been chosen because we want to emphasize the community that we are building in our classroom and the links that our curriculum will make to the world outside the classroom. We are now ready to delve more deeply into concepts and competencies from the curriculum and continue our journey together.

2 Standard Reading Assessment

Purposes of Assessment

Assessment *of* learning: to report progress
Assessment *for* learning: to choose a class focus for instruction
Assessment *as* learning: to set personal learning goals

Assessment serves several purposes. In the past, most assessment was assessment *of* learning, with information collected to use in reporting out progress. Once the information had been collected, the teacher sighed or celebrated, and then moved on. Although assessment *of* learning is important, it is not the assessment that most affects student achievement. That would be assessment *for* learning.

Assessment to Promote Student Achievement

In assessment *for* learning, the primary purpose is to gather information about how students are doing in their learning in order to choose a class focus: to decide what to teach next. The teacher looks for patterns in the students' work, sees what they are able to do and what is missing, and uses this information to design instruction. A series of questions guides these decisions. Here are the first three:

1. What can my students do?
2. What is missing?
3. What do I need to teach?

Assessment for learning is a cyclical process. Once the information from the assessment has been gathered, analyzed, and used to design further instruction, teaching continues, fuelled by the new information. In four to six weeks, the assessment process is repeated. This return to the assessment allows teachers to see whether or not their teaching has made a difference, particularly in the focus area. The new results are analyzed, focusing on two more questions:

4. Did my teaching make a difference?
5. If it did, what is my next class goal? If not, what will I do differently in order to assist my students in learning?

Another purpose of assessment is assessment *as* learning. In this assessment, the focus is on descriptive feedback. The student is involved in analyzing his or her results and uses this information to set personal learning goals. Thus, each student is aware of and works towards the whole class focus, but also identifies a pertinent personal goal. After the first assessment for learning, each student sets a goal. After the second assessment, each student poses these questions:

- Did I achieve my goal?
- If not, what else can I do to improve towards this goal?
- If I did, what is my new goal?

This assessment-to-instruction sequence is repeated throughout the school year. Students and teachers work together to explicitly figure out what students can do, what they want to do, and how they are going to accomplish this, monitoring students' progress towards meeting curricular expectations.

Helping Students Assess Their Developing Skills

Based on research related to literacy learning and formative assessment (Schnellert, Butler, and Higginson 2008), British Columbia's Performance Standards for Reading describe three aspects of reading: strategies, comprehension, and response/analysis. They describe expected student performance in reading at each grade for March/April of the calendar year, on a four-point scale:

1 not yet within expectations
2 minimally meeting expectations
3 fully meeting expectations
4 exceeding expectations

What rubrics do you use to guide your instruction?

We code student samples by highlighting the descriptors in the grade-level performance standard that best match the student's work.

We use classroom texts, newspapers, and magazines as texts for our students in Grades 7 to 10.

The Standard Reading Assessment is one of the pieces in our assessment portfolio. It is used to monitor students' independent application of the skills and strategies we are teaching in our reading program. These assessments occur regularly and are used to keep us and our students informed of their performance and their progress.

In the Standard Reading Assessment, students read and respond to a common text. As the students are completing their response sheets, the teacher or teachers move around the room and listen to each student read a short passage from the text. Students choose which part of the text they will read and have an opportunity to practise it before reading to the teacher. As the student reads, the teacher keeps a modified running record of how the student is reading. This running record is recorded on the student's own text copy and is returned to the student with a compliment about the reading, written right on the sheet.

We believe it is important that the classroom teacher and the learning resource teacher work together on this process whenever possible. If they are working together, a class of 30 students can be assessed in 45 minutes in the elementary years or 60 minutes in the middle years and in secondary classrooms. The two teachers can then sit down with the student samples, code them, and together choose a class focus, based on patterns found in the student samples. This process, at first, may take longer than 45 or 60 minutes, but time required for the administration and the coding becomes less as the teachers become more experienced with the process. One of the many benefits of this collaboration is common goal setting. Doing this is particularly important for students at-risk, as it provides for them a more consistent program with both teachers reinforcing common goal areas.

Having a ready supply of good materials is an asset. Initially, the texts we choose for our intermediate students come from *Reading and Responding — Evaluation Resources for Your Classroom* (Jeroski and Brownlie 2006). There are poems, information articles, and narrative texts to use for assessment at each grade level. As we continue with the assessments, however, we find ourselves writing some of the material and choosing other material from classroom texts, brochures, magazines, and newspapers — any material that seems appropriate to help us determine the strengths and areas in need of strengthening of our group of readers. We usually begin the year using information texts for our assessments. We find that more students are challenged with reading information, so it is critical that we direct our teaching towards this area. In middle and secondary schools, where several teachers share the same group or grade of students, the assessment completed in one class can provide an instructional goal across subject areas.

A Range of Response Tasks

The response tasks are open-ended, so practice with them supports student learning. Often, the response task is kept the same for several assessments while the text changes. The student responses may be drawn, written, spoken, or a combination. The assessment is of reading, not of writing. By removing the "answer in complete sentences" directive, the focus is on reading as thinking. There are four different response tasks that we choose from for intermediate, middle, and secondary students:

1. a) Using your ideas, images, and feelings, show me you understand.
   b) What did you notice about your work today?

2. a) What have you liked or learned in this piece?
   b) What two questions would you like to ask the author?
   c) How does what you read connect with what you know?
   d) What do you think the author wanted you to remember from this text?
   e) What should I notice about your work today?

3. Make notes to show that you understand this piece of text. Comment on how you got along with reading and responding.

4. a) Connections: How does what you read connect with what you already knew?
   b) Summarizing: Choose a way to show the main ideas and details in what you read.
   c) Inferencing: Read between the lines to find something that you believe to be true, but that isn't actually said. Explain your reasoning.
   d) Vocabulary: Here are three challenging words from the text: [identify the words]. Explain what you think they mean.
   e) Reflecting: Was this easy or hard to understand? How did you help yourself understand?

With primary students, we have used the questions from #2 above or the following three prompts:

1. What did you read about?
2. List, web, draw, or write about what you learned.
3. Was this easy or hard to read? Why? How did you help yourself?

The Assessment Process

1. *Previewing the Text.* The teacher reads the title of the passage and sets the stage for the topic or genre of the text by brainstorming with the students what they know about it. Before beginning to read aloud, the teacher previews the response sheet to help set a purpose for reading. When using the first response — "Using your ideas, images, and feelings, show me you understand" — the teacher brainstorms with the class for what this could look like. If working with primary students, the teacher ensures that the children understand the choices in listing, webbing, drawing, and writing when using that response format.

Practice with common, open-ended responses supports student learning.

It is important, especially at the beginning of the year, to establish what students think they have permission to do in demonstrating an understanding.

2. *Silent Reading and Responding.* A passage and a response sheet are chosen and distributed to each student. The teacher invites the students to read the passage, circling words with which they are unfamiliar.

3. *Oral Reading.* As the students are reading and responding, the teacher moves from student to student and listens to them read. The student chooses a piece of the text already practised. The teacher takes the student's piece of text, gives the student a clean copy, and records the student's reading moves. The teacher records the following:

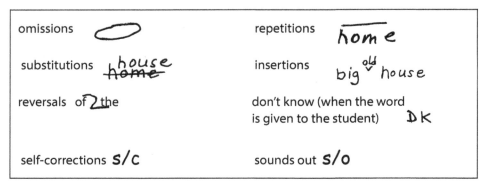

Prior to leaving the student, the teacher jots a quick compliment about the reading on the student's page.

4. *Collecting.* Once all students have had an opportunity to give an oral reading sample and have completed their responses, all the papers (both the student copy of the text and the student response sheet) are collected for coding.

The response sheets below address the fourth response task outlined on page 27.

Name: Rachelle   Date:

Text Title: Parties without Presents

Response Sheet - Intermediate

1. (Connections)- How does what you read, connect with what you already knew? I know that lots of people have so much stuff that on their birthdays they say "You don't have to buy me a present, I already have a lot of things!" That my mom and dad say the exact same thing but they still to it.

2. (Summarizing)- Choose a way to show the main ideas and details in what you read.

- Another one said a b-day without presents!?
- One of the geusts really wanted to pick a present
- What geust thought
- I guess they really have a good Idea!
- Parties without presents
- No Presents!!!?
- 2,500$ (USA 1,900?)
- Had B-days joint so money to raise!
- They rasied 500$ one time then.
- rasing money!!
- I don't get it why wouldn't a kid want presents!!!?
- who ever thought of that must be very smart!

3. (Inferencing)- Read between the lines to find something that you believe to be true, but that isn't actually said. Explain your reasoning.
I think that birthbay was held somewhere in Canada because it said the Canadian money part first then in U.S.A. I also think that not all the geusts brot money and a small gift.

4. (Vocabulary:) Thee are 3 challenging words from the text. Explain what you think they mean.

gadget   means two things together

joint   means something that helps you do something.

endangered   means a thing or animal that is almost gone!!!

How did you go about figuring out these words? What strategies did you use?
Well, First I read then when I found one of the words I would stop find out what it ment then write the meaning! It really wasnt hard.

5. (Reflecting)- Was this easy or hard? How did you help yourself understand?
Well, I think the hard part was the smarry but everything else was easy!

5. *Including and Supporting.* All students are included in this assessment, but support is added as necessary for beginning ELLs and students with severe reading difficulties. One of the teachers, for example, may work with a small group and read the passage aloud. Sometimes, students are asked to simply read one or two paragraphs, circle the words they know, and draw a picture or diagram of what they believe the passage is about.

We record the text and date of each assessment on a copy of the grade-appropriate Reading Performance Standard. Since this is descriptive scoring, the rubric is not used to assign a number or a rank. Teachers highlight words and phrases on the Standard that they have evidence for, based on what they have observed. The evidence (student text and student response sheet) is stapled to the Standard.

6. *Coding.* An overview page is created for each student. The text and date of each assessment over the year are noted on the page. Any information that has been gleaned from the student's oral reading sample, teacher interaction with the student, and the student's response sheet is recorded.

A different color is used for each assessment. At a glance, teachers, students, and parents can see areas of strength and of challenge. Over time, patterns emerge. By reporting period or the end of the year, this sheet will have a great deal of information on it about the student's reading performance in independent, text-related situations. The information can be read at a glance.

STRATEGIES	• reads words only; no meaning • dysfluent • waits for help on unfamiliar words • ignores text features	• relies on 1 or 2 specific strategies • careful, halting • uses context clues, if prompted	• adjusts strategies; reads for understanding • fluent • attempts to determine unfamiliar words • uses text features	• evaluates/questions own understanding • expressive • independently figures out unfamiliar words • uses text features effectively
COMPREHENSION	• work is incomplete; inaccurate • does not identify main ideas • unable to make notes • challenged with specific vocabulary	• work is accurate, but lacks detail • identifies most main ideas • makes single notes with no categories • few inferences • makes some sense of specific vocabulary	• work is clear, detailed, complete • identifies main ideas • makes notes with categories • some inferences • more detailed sense of specific vocabulary	• work is precise and thoughtful • uses own words to express main ideas • makes organized, complete notes • makes inferences • identifies and explains specific vocabulary
ANALYSIS	• unable to connect new information with known	• makes general text-to-text and text-to-self connections	• connects new information in several ways	• connects and evaluates new information

Adapted from "Quick Scale, Grade 5 Reading for Information," *BC Performance Standards: Reading*

7. *Planning.* Once the responses have been coded, the teacher and the learning resource teacher search for class patterns. What does the class do well? What is a common area of need? Typically, we choose one focus related to strategies and one related to comprehension, response, or analysis. These become our goal areas. These goal areas are shared with the students so everyone knows what we are working towards. As well, as teachers, we decide on two or three specific teaching strategies that we will work on over the next four to six weeks to try to improve student learning in these two goal areas. These strategies are recorded, as shown in the following class example.

	Focus Area	Teaching Strategies
Strategies	• may need help choosing strategies	• daily think-aloud with focus on strategies • daily word-skill modeling and practice (5 min/day), focus on prefixes, suffixes, root words and their connections
Comprehension	• main ideas and details	• collaborative summary • what's important and why • power paragraph

As students gain experience using Performance Standards, they can go on to share their progress with their parents at student-led conferences.

8. *Sharing.* It is important that the students are also involved in this feedback cycle of assessment. Often, after the first assessment, we do not have individual conferences with students about their performance on the assessment. We share the information about the class's performance as we use student samples to collaboratively build criteria. After the second assessment, when students have had an opportunity to engage in this form of response and have participated in focused, deliberate teaching, we conference with students, emphasizing their progress towards the specific class focus and helping them set personal goals.

Using the Information

Assessments are worth doing when they give teachers information to inform their practice. We need to see that our teaching is making a difference. The following scenarios are typical of the action taken as a result of information collected on the class assessment.

1. Building Criteria for Powerful Response

When choosing student response samples, try to include a variety of representations, such as web, paragraph, and picture. Choose samples because they are powerful in some way: they have achieved some of what constitutes more sophisticated reading behavior.

From time to time, the teacher chooses five or six student response samples. The samples are shown to the class, one at a time, with a comment like this: "I have chosen a variety of your responses to use as samples. These samples will help us build criteria for what really works or what is powerful in this type of response." The students are asked, "What strikes you as powerful about this sample?" or "What do you notice that really works in this sample?" The questions are positive, and only positive comments are accepted. These comments are recorded for the class to see. Once all the response samples have been reviewed, the teacher and class review their comments and reorganize them into a more coherent form as a set of criteria.

The criteria are posted to guide other text responses the students might make over the next four to six weeks to gain practice in a variety of supported and independent contexts before being assessed again. This list of criteria is also used by students to self-assess their responses from the assessment and to set a personal reading goal for the next month. Goals will vary greatly from student to student, but each student chooses a goal within the context of the class goals and graded curriculum expectations. Patterns noticed in the class's reading performance indicate direction for teaching in the next four to six weeks.

In the following samples, students in Grades 6 and 7 have responded to an information text "Pollution Blamed for Seal Deaths" (Jeroski and Brownlie 2006, Grade 6). They were given this prompt: "Using your ideas, images, and feelings, show me you understand."

In the criteria-building session, Ronnie's is the first sample. The students notice that Ronnie has shown *cause and effect* (the factories and the toxic wastes in the water) and *emotion* (the seal cub calling out to the mother).

Michelle's is the second sample, and the students add *main idea and some good details from the article* and *summary* to the list.

> Pollution Blamed For Seal Deaths   Michelle
>
> Because of pollution, about 7000 harbour seals have died. In West Germans waters, another 2000 have died. ∧ Each year, 400,000 tonnes of oil leak into the ocean. Too much toxic waste are dumped in the ocean. Scientist have found tumors and lesions in fish, caused by the toxic waste.
>
> This has been one of the worst ever ecological disasters

Finally, Anita's sample is shown. The students notice her *details from the text* and the *relationships* shown on her web.

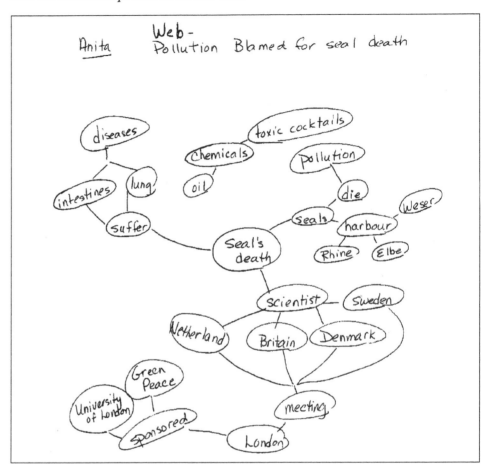

The criteria list that is posted includes ideas like these:

- main idea and some specific details
- emotional connection
- how ideas fit together — their relationship to each other
- extending — thinking beyond the text
- cause and effect
- summary — be sure we can tell you have read the text, not just used your own ideas

2. Small-Group Support

A few days after the assessment, either the classroom teacher or the learning resource teacher gathers the students who had difficulty with reading the text or with a particular response, along with the text that they read, and their responses. During this small-group mini-lesson, teacher and students look at the words circled, discussing how to say these words and possible meanings. Next, they choose a part of the text to read aloud together, discussing, as they read, the connections they are making and what they are thinking about.

If a small group of students are experiencing difficulty with reading the text or with generating a particular response, these students can rework the challenging part of the assessment with support.

Finally, they return to the response. If the students had been asked to respond to more than one question, only one is chosen as a focus during this conference.

The question is read aloud and ways to respond to the question are discussed. When the teacher is confident that this entire group of students is able to respond to the question, the students address it again. These responses are coded and charted with the symbol *WS*, to indicate what the students could do *with support*. This not only allows the students explicit, direct instruction for the desired achievement, but also boosts their confidence, because they have now witnessed themselves as better able to perform. The teacher has specific information on where the students were experiencing difficulty and on what strategies were effective in supporting them. These, then, are applied, as appropriate, in a variety of contexts in the next four to six weeks.

In this sample, notice the change in Christine's response to a prompt from a Grade 5 selection "Flying" (Jeroski and Brownlie 2006, Grade 5): "Using your ideas, feelings, and images, show me in writing that you understand the story."

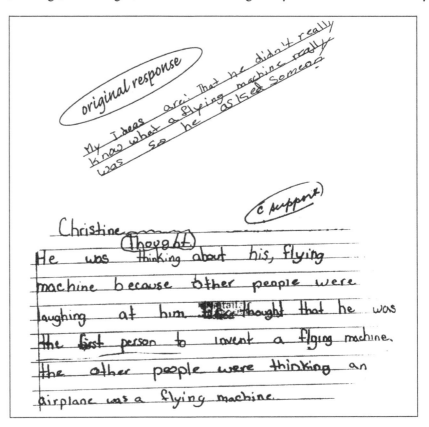

3. Vocabulary

Students, especially English language learners or those for whom the text is very challenging, do not benefit from having long lists of miscued words. A personal list should not exceed 10 words. Students become very proud of their accomplishments when they recognize their growing independence with vocabulary.

As we code the responses, miscued words are noted. Individual lists can be dated and charted on the student's sheet. The words can be read and talked about in small groups with the learning resource teacher. Sometimes the students practise these new "challenge" words with partners. A class list of miscued words is also kept. In mini-lessons of 5 to 10 minutes over the next two weeks, the teacher returns to these words and studies them with the class. This study includes strategies for decoding the words — such as phonics and structural analysis — and strategies for making sense of the words within the context of the text.

4. Preparation for the Next Standard Reading Assessment

We find it useful to use the same response questions and the same genre of text at least two or three times in a row. Doing so allows the students to directly apply the skills and strategies that they have been taught, based on the results of the last assessment.

At the beginning of the next assessment, the students revisit the criteria developed from the five or six student response samples. This assessment will use a different reading passage, perhaps a different genre of text, or different response questions. To begin the next assessment, the students and teacher review the criteria and decide which of those items listed will be important to consider in this assessment. They may add or delete items. The students are also reminded of their personal reading goal. They are invited to think about the criteria prior to reading: "As you begin to demonstrate your understanding, what will you keep in mind?" Following the assessment, they return to their response and reflect on these questions, the first referenced to the criteria: "What should you notice that I did today?" "What will I keep in mind for next month?"

A webcast details how to use the Standard Reading Assessment to inform instruction. "Literacy in the Middle Years — Part 1," by Faye Brownlie, is available at www.insinc.com/ministryofeducation/. It was first presented 7 October 2004.

The Standard Reading Assessment is just one part of our classroom assessment program. We aim to administer it five or six times a year, to monitor the changes in our students' performance, to see the impact of our teaching and whether or not we need to adjust our teaching. We find that using this assessment on a regular basis helps us keep our instruction aligned with the needs of our students. This alignment improves our effectiveness as teachers and reminds us to keep our focus constantly on our students.

3 Getting Strategic with Strategies

From the beginning of the year, we focus on creating learning experiences that help all of our students grow and succeed. For us this means determining which skills our students need to develop while learning about important and often new concepts. We plan based on assessment results.

When classroom and learning resource teachers work together to use and adapt strategies for students in the classroom, it becomes easier to see what aspects of the content students are understanding, as well as which curricular competencies they are developing and which ones they need more experience with. When two or more teachers plan and work together, there are always more ideas for creating and adapting learning sequences and strategies to meet the needs of the diverse learners in the classroom. Learning resource teachers can help classroom teachers choose a strategy or approach that matches the competency a class needs to develop, can help match the strategy to the text or activity that will be used, and can adapt the strategy for students who need more support.

Learning about Our Students as Learners

To plan lessons and units, we collect a great deal of information about our students early in the school year. As we get to know the students individually and what is unique and special about them, we strive to build a classroom community that honors and encourages diversity.

Student Learning Portfolios

We use the first term of school to help each student build a learning portfolio. A learning portfolio includes responses where students share their interests, strengths, and stretches, and the goals that they set; it also contains pieces completed throughout the term. We begin to explore the notion of each student documenting personal history. We also begin with a focus on personal writing (see Chapter 5).

Students collect the information from the various sources and put it into their learning portfolios. In one Grade 9 class, teacher Linda Watson helped her students create summaries of what they believed to be the most relevant and important information about themselves. Their learning profiles became the introductory section to their Humanities portfolios. At the end of each term the students updated their learning profiles based on the goals they had set, what they had done to achieve these goals, and what they had learned about themselves over the term. The portfolios were then handed in as part of their term's assessment. Having students create a personal summary of their learning as the introductory task in their portfolios helped Linda emphasize that reflection and goal setting are a priority in teaching and learning in her classroom.

Building a Class Profile

We encourage students to share their ideas in a variety of ways, such as words, pictures, charts, and diagrams.

On the Getting to Know You graphic organizer (pages 37 and 38) is a set of prompts we have used extensively in Grades 4 through 10 classrooms to begin the process of building a class profile. The front of the two-sided organizer looks at strengths and interests. It asks students to tell us, from their point of view, what we really need to know about them. The back of the graphic organizer looks at the intensely private matter of fears. Getting to Know You is the first step in our assessment cycle for the year. Once we collect this information, we pull it out for every unit we plan.

Together, we examine the individual Getting to Know You sheets. We use this information about our students to guide our instruction. Grade 9 teacher Linda Watson and her LRT (learning resource teacher) partner took the same approach. They decided on three key areas of focus:

To develop a class profile, we use the Standard Reading Assessment (see Chapter 2), questionnaires about learning styles and multiple intelligences, and the Getting to Know You graphic organizer (pages 37 and 38).

1. They saw that students needed to focus their attention on interpreting specific tasks, setting goals, and reflecting on their efforts. To promote this, they built steps into lessons where students could both analyze the tasks they engaged in and determine what the tasks required of them.

2. They noted that the group was very active. To capitalize on their energy, they ensured that each phase of their lessons included opportunities for all students to talk. They also provided opportunities for students to represent their learning artistically and symbolically.

3. Aware of students who had a difficult time understanding, remembering, and/or applying new or abstract concepts, they were reminded to be explicit about key concepts in each lesson, so that they could modify tasks and activities as needed.

Class Profile: Humanities 9				
Dates:	**Strengths**	**Stretches**	**Interests/ Passions**	**GOALS**
Fall assessment for learning	– outgoing – self-aware – friendly – sense of humor – cooperative – enjoy reading – a positive atmosphere in the class	– risk taking to show their invisible knowledge – showing what they know – focusing, concentration – finding main ideas, details – making connections between what they know and what they read – some students with written output challenges – several students on modified programs	– movement (almost any kind) – cooking – creating things – visual art (some) – drama (some) – sports (some) – socializing	– create a safe classroom – help students understand the phases of teaching and learning – build students' self-regulated learning over the year **Decisions** – use the connecting, processing, and transforming phases to support risk taking, sharing, and self-advocacy – LRT co-teaching focus on reading in social studies and writing in English language arts during the first term – target making connections and finding the main idea – goal setting and self-assessment
Winter assessment for/ of learning				
Spring assessment for/ of learning				

Getting to Know You

Words That Describe Me	My Favorite Books/ Stories	Things I Like to Do with My Friends	My Favorite Activities When Alone	My Favorite Activities When with My Family
			Very Favorite: Other Activities:	
What I'm Very Interested In or Good At	Things I'd Like You to Know about Me (or what you need to know about me)	My Hopes and Dreams for Myself	The Easiest Ways for Me to Show What I Know	One Thing I'd Like to Get Better At in School This Year
			Very Favorite: Other Activities:	

Nicole Widdess, Linda Watson, and Leyton Schnellert

Pembroke Publishers © 2016 *Student Diversity*, 3rd ed., by Faye Brownlie, Catherine Feniak, Leyton Schnellert ISBN 978-1-55138-318-7

Getting to Know You (back)

Shhhhh!

My Greatest Fears . . .

Pembroke Publishers © 2016 *Student Diversity*, 3rd ed., by Faye Brownlie, Catherine Feniak, Leyton Schnellert ISBN 978-1-55138-318-7

Designing Lessons

Using teaching strategies makes learning new concepts fun, as students are more likely to participate in lessons that have engaging approaches. However, we also want our students to internalize the skills a teaching strategy targets and eventually apply these skills to their independent work. Once the lesson is over and the Smart Board or chalkboard has been erased, we want the students' memory of how and why we engaged them in the topic to stay with them. A good lesson sequence is a thing of beauty. When we link strategies and lessons together in a way that introduces students to new concepts and builds their skills over time, learning becomes fun and student performance increases.

We have key learnings from brain research in mind as we begin to design our lessons:

- Engage students by tapping into their interests and emotions.
- Show new information to students in a variety of ways.
- Provide students with different ways to show what they know. (Rose and Meyer 2002)

With this as the base, we add in our phases of teaching support for students' learning: connecting, processing, and transforming and personalizing. By planning with these key learning phases in mind we are able to ensure that we make accommodations for all of our learners in each phase.

Connecting — Making Connections That Last

Remember the phases of learning:
- connecting
- processing
- transforming and personalizing

Our first hurdle is engaging and motivating students. This phase of teaching and learning is all about connecting. To help students connect to the topic, we ask them to brainstorm what they know about the topic, begin a lesson with a simulation, have students sort and categorize vocabulary words, or pose some intriguing questions. There are many ways to help students get ready for new learning.

Processing — Actively Engaging with New Content

Once we help students activate their prior knowledge and set a purpose for their learning, we focus on developing and applying processing strategies. These strategies help students construct meaning, compare new knowledge to prior knowledge, and determine what is important. The modeling and practising of processing strategies teaches students to monitor their understanding while engaging with texts of all kinds (Tovani 2004; Wilhelm 2013).

Transforming and Personalizing — Creating Lasting Memories

After successfully making meaning of the text, students are encouraged to demonstrate their understanding. We focus on strategies that ask students to generate responses that deepen and personalize their understanding — to commit what they are learning to long-term memory.

Successfully creating powerful learning experiences for our diverse classes has led us to focus on incorporating teaching strategies that help students generate and use their own learning strategies. We help them understand what good readers, writers, and thinkers do, in order to help them become good readers, writers, and thinkers.

We advise doing this in three ways:

- Choose one or two key strategies to focus on at a time.
- Mentor students to acquire these strategies.
- Encourage students to create and adapt their own strategies once they are familiar with our expectations and we have spent time modeling ways to use a strategy.

- Choose your teaching strategies based on the skills you want to target.
- Explain to students how and why the teaching strategies you have chosen will help them.

By choosing just a few core teaching strategies each unit, we can ensure that students have an opportunity to master both the strategy and the thinking behind it. Our instructional planning becomes easier as we carefully choose a few strategies and weave them across the various subject areas and units of study. While a few students may need specific accommodations, all students can benefit from access to these approaches. With a learning resource teacher and classroom teacher working together, planning lessons that build the same competencies for all students, all students learn the same key strategies and then apply them to tasks where they can have success.

Starting with Information Text

In Linda Watson's cross-curricular Humanities class (see page 41), students started with non-fiction and moved into fiction. In Chapter 7, you will read how teacher Nicole Widdess moved from fiction to non-fiction in her slavery-themed unit.

As students move from grade to grade and from elementary to middle and secondary schools, they have to read more and more information text. By Grade 10, seven out of a typical student's eight classes require the student to work with a type of text unique to that subject area. With this in mind, we want to build awareness, confidence, and the skill sets of our students. Even before our initial assessment, we begin by setting up routines and a common lesson structure in our classes.

Reflecting on Strategy Focus

We deliberately explain to the students that each lesson has connecting, processing, and transforming and personalizing phases, and that each phase asks a reader to do different things. We often use the following questions to help us target specific strategies in each lesson.

- Connecting: How will we help our students get ready for new material?
- Processing: How will we help our students monitor their reading/learning?
- Transforming and Personalizing: How will we help our students use and integrate new information?

As we plan our lessons, we further refine our strategy focus by completing sentence stems for each phase.

Connecting: How will we help our students get ready for new material?

To help them activate prior knowledge, we'll show three objects and ask them to brainstorm what they know with a partner.

To help them

- set a purpose for reading/learning, we'll . . .
- activate prior knowledge, we'll . . .
- survey the text, we'll . . .
- set reading goals, we'll . . .

Processing: How will we help our students monitor their reading/learning?

To help them narrow their focus, we'll create a three-column chart with these prompts: What's most important? Why? and What do I wonder?

To help them

- narrow their focus, we'll . . .
- maintain their attention, we'll . . .
- be accountable for their thinking, we'll . . .
- identify important ideas, we'll . . .
- compare new knowledge to prior knowledge, we'll . . .
- ask questions, we'll . . .
- summarize or paraphrase, we'll . . .

Transforming and Personalizing: How will we help our students use and integrate new information?

To help them

To help them demonstrate understanding, organize information, and put ideas into their own words, we'll ask them to create a bumper sticker that summarizes the big idea of the text and includes an image or icon.
   To help them identify what they still need to learn, we'll ask them to write something they wonder about on a sticky note and post it on the board as they leave the classroom.

- demonstrate understanding in a variety of ways, we'll . . .
- organize information to remember it, we'll . . .
- identify what they still need to learn, we'll . . .
- put ideas into their own words, we'll . . .

We have found that in the fall students often ask us which phase of the lesson we are in; by the new year, though, students begin to name the lesson phase. If a lesson spans two or more classes, our students begin the class by reminding us which phase we were in the previous day. At the end of the year, we find it extremely gratifying to have students tell us which strategies they found most helpful and effective. We have found a wide range in students' preferred strategies. As a result, we build in opportunities for students to choose the strategy they would use, alter it, or create their own.

Planning with Reading Strategies in Mind

In our teaching, we use results from our Standard Reading Assessment (see Chapter 2) to choose and plan the strategy focus for each term.

For the Humanities 9 classes, Linda Watson and her LRT colleague chose to focus on determining importance when reading non-fiction, as both of Linda's classes struggled in this area on the Standard Reading Assessment. They decided that orienting the students to the features of information texts and introducing them to key concepts related to the big idea of change would be a perfect opportunity to practise these strategies. As they planned each lesson, they had to decide what the essential concepts were, what reading strategies would be targeted, and what teaching strategies would be used for students to connect with, process, and transform and personalize key content (see the Humanities 9 Planning Chart on page 43 and the Lesson Planning template, next page).

A full-size Lesson Planning line master is available at the end of the chapter.

Lesson Planning

Lesson: _____

Big Ideas or Key Concepts
Students will understand that . . .

Competencies or Strategies
Students will be able to . . .

Connecting	**Purpose:** Engagement. Activate prior knowledge. Predict content. Focus on a purpose for reading. **I/we will . . .**	How can I/we tap into students' interests, offer appropriate challenges, and increase motivation?
Processing	**Purpose:** Construct meaning. Monitor understanding. Process ideas. **I/we will . . .**	How will I/we help students interact with new ideas they encounter?
Transforming and Personalizing	**Purpose:** Process ideas. Apply knowledge. Reflect on thinking and learning. **I/we will . . .**	How can I/we provide learners with alternatives for demonstrating what they know?

Assessment

If students are engaged and I/we have modeled this well, I/we hope that they will . . .

1.   2.

3.   4.

Pembroke Publishers © 2016 *Student Diversity*, 3rd ed., by Faye Brownlie, Catherine Feniak, Leyton Schnellert ISBN 978-1-55138-318-7

Linda and her LRT colleague selected key strategies to use several times over the course of the unit or term. They put a star beside the strategy names in the Planning Chart. Their intention, in choosing and targeting certain strategies, was to give students an opportunity to practise these strategies with different texts, themes, and concepts while building their understanding of how a strategy helps them. Later in the year, students would select, adapt, and apply these strategies based on their analysis of a task.

Planning for Big Ideas

A good way to begin planning for the year is to identify engaging themes and units that cut across subject areas. In planning their Humanities 9 unit, Linda and her LRT colleague looked for the big ideas and key concepts in Social Studies and examined how these might fit with their English Language Arts (ELA) program. They determined one big idea for the year for Social Studies: Revolution Leads to Change. They then looked at the learning outcomes for Social Studies and for English Language Arts. It was not hard to plot these into the overall plan.

Linda and her teaching partner created a separate box on their Planning Chart for the reading strategy target (see the bottom row of the chart on page 43), to keep it in mind at all times. As they planned their lessons, considering the connecting, processing, and transforming and personalizing phases, they determined a variety of teaching strategies that could help them develop that reading strategy. They could not be too firm in their choice of skills and strategies, though, because they did not know how quickly the students would progress. This chart records what they did.

Humanities 9 Planning Chart
Big Ideas: Change, Power, Making a Difference

	Sept 13 to Oct 12	Mid-October	November	December
ELA Essential Learning Outcomes	(1) use language creatively to explore & express thoughts, ideas, feelings, experiences (2) work individually and in small groups and as a class to explore ideas, accomplish goals, maintain relationships, and build community	(1), (2), (3), (4) appreciate the power and beauty of language in their own creations and others (5) use rubrics and examples to assess own writing and language development	(1), (2), (3), (4), (5), (6) respond creatively, personally, and analytically in written, spoken, and graphic form to a variety of poetry, fiction, and non-fiction (7) apply knowledge and conventions of language in their written and spoken expression	(1), (2), (3), (4), (5), (6), (7), (8) generate a focused research topic, then gather & organize information for a variety of writing tasks (9) use language analytically to form, express, & defend an opinion on a controversial issue
English Language Arts	**Change theme** Writers Workshop: Memoirs **Activities/Strategies:** What Is Powerful Writing? Writing Our Basic Story Modeling Memoir Writing Cracking Open Your Memoir Commonplace Books*	**Change theme** Writers Workshop: Poetry **Activities/Strategies:** Heart Mapping (Heard) Where Poetry Hides (Atwell) Metaphors Similes Personification	**Heroes and Icons Theme** Reading Focus: Modeling *Introducing a new reading strategy using a poem* **Activities/Strategies:** What Do Good Readers Do? Think-Alouds Poetry Making Connections Goal Setting Author's Message Partner Talk	**Breaking through Labels Theme** From read-aloud to literature circles with same novel *Iqbal*, Francesco D'Adamo *Introducing a new reading strategy using picture book* **Activities/Strategies:** Visualizing 4 Quadrants Asking Questions Big Talk (small group) Big Talk Guidelines Creating Image/Symbol Quick Write
Social Studies Essential Learning Outcomes	(1) describe and assess the factors influencing the development of identity and the roots of social and cultural issues (2) gather, interpret, and evaluate information *ELA #3 develop and apply extensive strategies to anticipate, predict, and confirm meaning* Change Comes to Europe Modern Age, Fight for Democracy, English Civil War **Activities/Strategies:** Think-Alouds: Seeing reading Think-Pair-Share* Skimming and Scanning Mind Mapping* Writing in Role Who Are the Players?* Chunking Text* Finding & Using the Back Story	(1), (2), (3) examine the contributions of the French Revolution to the development of democratic concepts (4) define conflict and revolution **Activities/Strategies:** Critical Timeline* Think-Pair-Share* What's Important & Why* Who Are the Players?* Mind Mapping* 3 Sticky Notes = 3 Ideas Image/Icon Two-Column Notes*	(1), (2), (4), (5) identify and clarify a problem, issue, or inquiry (6) examine a variety of perspectives and defend a position on a controversial topic (7) define colonialism, imperialism, nationalism **Activities/Strategies:** What's Important & Why* Two-Column Journal* Acting Out a Player Critical Timeline* Reciprocal Teaching (Palinscar) Think-Pair-Share* Tableau	(1), (2), (4), (5), (6), (7) assess how economic systems contributed to the development of early Canada (8) plan, revise, document, defend, & present information **Activities/Strategies:** Think-Pair-Share* Two-Column Journal* Make a Prediction Think-Aloud What's Important & Why What's Fair (importance) Most Important and Why
Reading Strategies	Determining Importance	Determining Importance	Determining Importance Prediction & Making Connections	Determining Importance Asking Questions & Visualizing

Introducing a New Strategy

Before formally introducing a new strategy, we explain to the class how we have chosen it. We make our selection based on the results of the Standard Reading Assessment, which is outlined in Chapter 2.

When we introduce a new reading strategy that we want to focus on, we first model what the strategy looks like using a think-aloud. Over the next week or so, students get several opportunities to try out the strategy in fiction and non-fiction texts in our thematic units. To begin, we chunk the text into smaller pieces so we can stop and explain our thinking. Doing this helps both teachers and students to be explicit about what they are doing.

A copy of the text is projected. With the text in view for everyone and pen in hand, we share what we are thinking and record it on the Smart Board.

The following sequence is a sample of the lessons taught in Linda's classroom.

Change and the Industrial Revolution

Connecting Phase: This phase promotes engagement, activates prior knowledge, prompts students to predict content, and puts a focus on a purpose for reading.
Strategy: Think-Pair-Share
1. Make this invitation: "Think of an invention or form of technology that has changed the way you live your life."
2. In partners, students discuss examples as the teachers move around the class, giving support as needed.
3. Create a T-chart on the board:

Big Changes in 21st/22nd Century	Big Changes from 1700 On

4. Have groups discuss their inventions. List on the board. Draw out what the big change was and put in chart.

Processing Phase: In this phase, students identify possible changes and support their choices.
Strategy: 3 Sticky Notes = 3 changes
1. Read the first chunk from the text out loud; put a sticky note by a possible change.
2. Discuss your choice with the class.
3. Read the next chunk of text, then invite students to place a sticky note beside an idea in this section of the text and share their thinking with a partner.
4. Present two more chunks of information, and have students read to identify two more changes, placing their sticky notes by them.
5. Debrief as a class. Fill in the second half of the T-chart together.

Transforming and Personalizing Phase: Students process ideas and reflect on their thinking and learning.
Strategy: Quick Write
1. Review criteria for quick writes.
2. Say: "Using what we've just read, describe what you think the Industrial Revolution is all about."
3. Give this direction: "Make a prediction using webs, words, pictures, charts, or some other format. Show me your best thinking."

Over time we move from teacher modeling and the guiding of student skill use to collaborative use of the strategy in texts of students' own choice. We use literature and information circles as opportunities to apply key reading strategies in a real-world manner.

In her classroom, over several months, Linda moved from modeling to partner work to literature circles, with her LRT colleague joining her once a week to co-teach an anchor lesson. There had been ample practice of comprehension skills and strategies during reading activities in the fall. In the winter, the students came prepared for their conversations, knowing what strategy they needed to focus on. With a few key ideas and responses in mind, they used the Say Something strategy (see Chapter 7) to start their conversations.

The Literature Circles chart on page 46 illustrates how Linda and her LRT partner built from an anchor text, *Iqbal*, to picture books and then to a choice of novels, all related to the same concepts and big ideas. The reading strategies

Linda moved from modeling a strategy with one text to introducing literature circle conversations, to encouraging independent application with students' own literature book choices. These developments are reflected in the chart "Literature Circles" on page 46.

that students used and developed arose from the goals and plans made for the fall (see the Class Profile on page 36). Once Linda and her LRT colleague had identified the big ideas that they wanted her students to explore, it was easy to plan out lessons that helped students develop proficiency with the strategies of content-area reading while exploring a key concept related to a big idea over the course of a unit of study. By using the results from the Standard Reading Assessment, Linda and her LRT colleague were able to choose a strategy to focus on for a month to six weeks. They saw students become more proficient with this strategy because they had time to master it.

Teaching Reading in the Early Years

Young readers deserve to be surrounded with text that they want to read, to have opportunities to read and to talk to one another about their reading, to respond purposefully to their reading, and to see themselves as readers as they become readers.

Joy and Success from the Outset

Lisa Schwartz believes that it is important for learners in Grades 1 and 2 to experience joy and success as readers from the beginning of the school year. To find out where the students are on their reading journey, she begins the year with a performance-based reading assessment (see Chapter 2). This information helps her set goals for her teaching and for the students' learning. This assessment and daily reading with the students help her establish small reading groups and help her determine which reading strategies will become the explicit instructional focus. Lisa understands that the students need time to practise the strategies they are being taught.

Opportunities for this practice occur in the literacy centres which are established in September. This particular pattern for literacy centres allows all students to be successful, to have choice, to collaborate with others, to do lots of reading, and to experience joy and success while reading. Included, as well, in the 75-minute teaching block is whole-class explicit teaching of skills in context, a 1:1 reading conference to choose "just right" books, and a group reflection on what worked in their reading, what they enjoyed, and what they learned.

Taking a Collaborative Approach

Today, Lisa is a district literacy consultant. In this illustration of how to teach reading, she is co-teaching with Terra McKenzie in Terra's combined Grades 1 and 2 class. They have prepared their literacy centres and introduced them to the students over several days, introducing only one or two centres per day. For a literacy centre to be successful, students need to be secure in their knowledge of the possibilities of the centre, the expectations of the centre, and how to take care of the centre (how to take it out, clean it up, and put it back).

A Lesson Involving Literacy Centres

The lesson begins with the students seated on the carpet. They have been naming reading strategies throughout the month and they review them

Literature Circles
Topic: The Industrial Revolution and Child Slavery
Big Ideas: Change, Making Connections

	Lesson 1 Focus: Making connections	Lesson 2 Focus: Making connections	Lesson 3 Focus: Collecting info for conversations	Lessons 4-10 Focus: Making images in your mind
Connecting	Read aloud: *Iqbal* ➤ Moving into literature circles with a common novel - Read chapter 1 of *Iqbal* - Make predictions and connections using the title and cover - Share predictions and questions with a partner and then the class	Read aloud: *Iqbal* - Discuss important connections homework to refresh memory of chapter 1 - Remind students that focus is on text:text, text:self and text:world connections - Revisit the book talk criteria	Read aloud: *Aunt Harriet's Underground Railroad in the Sky* ➤ Introducing a new strategy - Set purpose of collecting ideas for literature circle conversations - Using the first page of the story, model the collection of images and descriptive/powerful language	Read aloud: Continue use of 4 Quadrants and group conversations with *Iqbal*
Processing	Read aloud chapter and stop 3 times to allow students to jot connections down in their logs	Read aloud chapter 2 and stop 3 times to allow students to jot connections down in their logs	- Ask students to do the same from second page - Look for example that students could add to the 4 Quadrants on the overhead - Repeat with next two pgs - Model one emotion - Repeat and add wonder	Explore using Sticky notes Double-entry journals Listen, Sketch, Draft
Transforming/ Personalizing	- Share connections in small groups - Generate criteria – what makes a good book conversation	New groups of 4 - book conversations Revise the criteria in small groups, students assess selves: one strength, one goal for next time	- Finish up book with asking student to add to quadrants that need more examples - exit slip	Using illustrations from picture books to introduce questioning
Homework	*Quick write – explain 3 important connections that you made*	*Quick write – explain 3 important connections that you made*	*N/A*	*Targeted reflections – explain which images were most powerful and why*

	Lessons 11–15 Focus: Making connections	Lesson 16 Focus: Making connections	Epilogue Focus: Comprehension activity	Moving into new books Focus: Making images in your mind
Connecting	Read aloud: *Iqbal* - Book talks – introduce students to the industrial revolution literature circles titles *Midnight Is a Place* *The Grave* *Street Child* *Crispin* *Oliver Twist* Listen, Sketch, Draft is a chance to show what you can do – make sure you have all 4 parts of the quad and your connections	Read aloud Have students decide on top three books for industrial revolution Brainstorm as a group what else can be added to the discussion criteria	Read aloud: *Iqbal* Focus on creating an image that represents Iqbal (relate to the symbol work done in Social Studies). You may wish to represent Iqbal as a symbol of the battle again child slavery and/or violence	Send into new groups based on book choice Explain use of Sticky notes Double-entry journals Listen, Sketch, Draft Evaluation will be based on discussion and responses
Processing	Read aloud chapter and stop 3 times to allow students to jot images, words, wonders and feelings down	Read aloud chapter 15 - student choice for "note-taking"	- Ask students to listen for details to support the development of their symbol	Say Something strategy
Transforming/ Personalizing	- Book groups - How does hearing about others' images change your thinking?	Book discussion groups Students assess themselves: one strength as a group, one goal for next time	Criteria: - you can use any media in your work - must relate to feelings and emotions - make the viewer wonder - must have combination of images or one detailed icon/symbol	Group assessment
Homework	*How does hearing about others' images change your thinking?*	*Quick write – what did you notice in this chapter? How did you represent your thinking? Why?*	*Work on image*	*Two-column journal*

together. Now Lisa presents a text with several words covered up. As they read together from this shared text, they stop at each covered word and try to determine what the word could be. As they are predicting the word, they are also explaining what strategy they are using. Lisa hears several responses, then reveals the initial letters of the word, and the students adjust or confirm their prediction. They stay together on the carpet, practising these reading skills in context for only 10 to 12 minutes. They review the strategies they will use as they are reading independently today.

Terra reminds the students of the day's literacy centres: Read Like a Scientist, Read Like a Rock Star, Elephant and Piggy, Read Like an Artist, and Read Like a Writer. The students are in assigned heterogeneous groups of four or five. They will work in every literacy centre today, with about 10 to 12 minutes in each.

While the students are in their centres, Lisa and Terra take on different roles. Terra monitors the groups and moves from group to group, listening to students read, coaching, supporting, and extending as needed. After 10 minutes, she gives a minute cleanup warning, then moves the groups to the next centre. Lisa calls students to her one at a time. She has collections of levelled text with her. Based on her current knowledge of the child, she chooses three or four books of different levels and different interests and asks the child to find a book that he thinks would be a good choice. They read the book together, with Lisa noticing the child's strategies and talking to him about what he is reading and what attracted him to the book. Once she has a better idea of a good fit book, she presents another selection of books around the same level and the child chooses three "just right" books. These books are then placed in a Browsing Bag. Once Lisa has conferenced with all the students, Browsing Bags can become another literacy centre (or another literacy activity at a different time of the day).

As the students rotate through each centre, the teachers have a mini-conference with each student. They call the class together for a 10-minute reflection on the lesson. Students are asked first about what worked well in their literacy centres; they are also prompted to outline any challenges they had and how they solved them. They then are invited to share something they learned from their reading or from a book which they think someone else in the class might enjoy. The carpet time is purposeful and joyful. These students are excited about their reading. They are excited to share information they are learning. They have had an extended reading time with different tasks providing multiple opportunities to read. The level of engagement has been high.

Real Reading throughout the Year

As the year continues and the students gain more independence, Terra invites her learning resource teacher to join the literacy centre time, and as a consultant, Lisa moves on to another class. The literacy centres change from time to time, and the time at each centre is extended as the students become better able to work for longer periods of time. The reading is authentic. There are no separate skills sheets for practice. Eyes are on text, and students are making meaning. Most important, all students of all skill levels are engaged in real reading and the teachers have time to meet with them in small groups and individually to nudge them along in their reading journey.

Browsing Bags are personal collections of "just right" books that young students want to read and can read. These "just right" choice books can be read independently, with a friend, at home, or with an adult. The books change as the students are ready for new texts or new topics.

Reading Strategies
- Look at the picture.
- Ask, "Does this make sense?"
- Go back and reread.
- Look at the beginning of the word and think about what makes sense.
- Find a little word inside the bigger word.
- Skip the word, finish the sentence, then reread and see what makes sense.
(Johnson and Keier 2010)

Literacy Centre	Materials	Activity
Read Like a Scientist	"I wonder" AND information text Clipboards and pencils	Read to find out interesting information. Record something you want to remember, if you want, on the clipboard. Bring recorded information to the reflection time to be shared.
Read Like a Rock Star	Microphones Song books and poems	Read the poems and songs together, practising for a performance.
Elephant and Piggy	Collection of books by Mo Willems that have been read together in the class	Browse the books, retelling stories from the pictures and reading challenging, but more familiar text.
Read Like an Artist	Drawing books and pages of drawing directions	Read the instructions (pictures and words) and draw different people, animals, and objects.
Read Like a Writer	Teacher-made joke books Blank mini-books and pencils	Read the jokes to one another. Make new jokes.

A Student-Created Joke

"What do you call a skeleton that lies on it's grave? Lazybones."

Here, a student is reading like an artist by drawing creatures based on directions.

Formative Assessment in Math

Building in opportunities for students to work with a mathematical concept, in this case, measurement, allows teachers to uncover what students know.

Because of the diversity in our classrooms, assessment needs to be built in from the beginning. In planning a unit on measurement for his Grade 3 class, Ray Appel began by first finding out what his students knew. He also needed to know the outcomes (content, curricular competencies) in order to establish goals and possible routes for his students' learning journey. As Ray was planning, he stayed away from writing "By the end of the lesson the students will be *able* to . . . ," since he did not yet know what they were able to do. Rather, as he planned early on and considered assessment, he used the phrase "By the end of the lesson(s) the students will have had the *opportunity* to . . ."

Understanding measurement, the focus of this math unit, does not just happen during a two-week period. To help all learners, Ray incorporated the concept of measurement early in the year with daily oral language, highlighting specific time events, as well as journaling with measurement in mind. He knew that getting in touch with the learning resource teacher early on was crucial. When both the classroom and learning resource teachers are reinforcing key measurement competencies using words, numbers, and pictures across settings, struggling learners are better able to build a solid formation. In this example, the learning resource teacher was able to reinforce Ray's learning goals and his language as they worked together to support all learners.

When the time was right for examining the concept of measurement in a deeper manner with the whole class, three columns — Always, Sometimes, Never — were drawn on the whiteboard (see photo below).

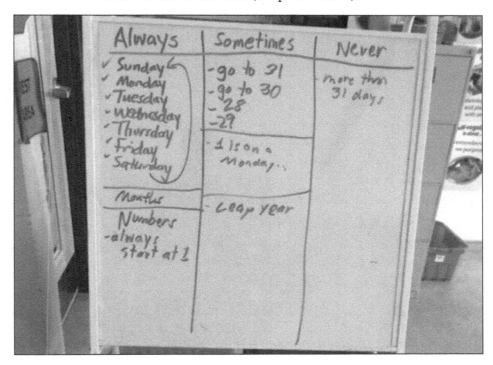

This began the process of learning more about what the students knew. Ray and his class added to the triple-column chart as they moved deeper into the concept of measurement and time. He utilized pair-share conversations to enable students to support each other. If a student was struggling, there was someone nearby who might have some ideas.

Ray believes in giving a lot of wait time after posing a prompt or question. Waiting three or more seconds on some of the prompts gives all learners a chance to formulate ideas. It also reinforces that intelligence is more than having a hand up first. Sometimes, pondering, considering, and weighing options is better than an instant response. For example, when a student suggested that all months have 31 days, classmates wondered if that idea would fit under "Always," "Sometimes," or "Never." The goal at this point was to move all learners from not yet meeting expectations to meeting expectations, while they learned from one another in the guided sharing time.

Finding Diverse Routes to Learning

Calendar Prompts

My special day is . . .
One week before is . . .
Two days before is . . .
Three days after is . . .

To follow up on the rich discussion, a simple blank calendar was created to help the variety of students in the classroom. Each student was going to create a calendar month and then select a personal special day. As well, each student had a series of prompts that would elicit different responses. As students worked on their personal calendars, Ray had a chance to extend their thinking, guide their work, and encourage thoughtful reflection. The discussion, risk taking, and active sharing of what they knew encouraged students to share the concept rather than the answer.

All the students placed the calendar organizer on their desks. Ray went around the room and told them where to start the first day (you'll begin *1* on a Monday; you'll begin on a Thursday). He was careful to avoid giving students who sat beside each other the same start day. As for students selecting their special day, he wanted them to choose a different day than the students around them (see the photos showing three students' calendar months).

You can see that one student started the month on a Sunday, another on a Wednesday, and another on a Monday. Two of the special days are the same (19), but the other has a different special day. The solutions to the prompts reveal a wonderful variety of understandings! Some students were able to write ordinal indicators (st, nd, rd, th); others wrote the days of the week, while others were able to print the name of the day and the number.

Just like the learners in the classroom, Ray had a variety of places to begin, as well as varied responses to the prompts at the bottom of the organizer. Even the student who struggled the most had success, making a calendar with 31 or fewer days, in proper sequential order, in the correct boxes, days of the week beginning and ending in the right places. In contrast to a fill-in-the-blank approach, where items are usually right or wrong, there was initial success for everyone.

Building from Formative Assessment

To begin the discussion the following day, Ray projected the variety of samples for the students to discuss. As a class, they helped each other, asked questions, cleared up misunderstandings, and acknowledged the variety of learning. Ray had copied the same organizer on both sides of the paper so that students could see the first side as a possible draft. After the discussion on the carpet, a number of students wanted to refine and reorganize what they had done. Now it was time to focus on some of the *criteria* that permeated this project: using rich *vocabulary* (before, during, after) to describe specific events in time, creating a *sequential, ordered* calendar, being able to share orally what *made sense*, as well as being able to *estimate* future timelines and events.

Meanwhile, Ray had looked again at the outcomes, content, and curricular competencies in order to see the common benchmarks for the class. It helped him (and the class) stay focused and guided his language on evaluation and reporting. Ray continued to think about the kinds of learning evidence that might illustrate "approaching," "meeting," and "exceeding" expectations. At this stage, he found it invaluable to show many student samples and have the students share. Again, the goal was to move all learners towards meeting and exceeding expectations, while they learned from one another in a collaborative and natural way.

A Winning Team

Exploring specific concepts in a variety of ways (journal writing, with hands-on, open-ended tasks and oral sharing), as well as the classroom teacher working closely with a learning resource teacher, forms a foundation that helps to support all learners in the classroom. Thinking, planning, and incorporating assessment early on and throughout the process helps all students see assessment as less linear and as more of an ongoing weaving of a rich tapestry: a weaving of descriptive feedback, criteria for success, personal and group reflection, rich questions, and opportunities to use what has been learned.

Many classroom teachers find collaboratively planning units with their learning resource teachers to be an immense support. In co-planning units, two teachers can better address student diversity and support and extend the learning of all students. Co-planning how to develop key content and competencies within and across lessons creates engaging learning opportunities for all. The classroom teacher brings her content expertise and knowledge of the key concepts required to understand the subject. The learning resource teacher contributes a background in reading strategies and skills and supporting students at-risk. Together, this is a winning team.

You might prefer to start by co-planning a single lesson sequence. You could use the Lesson Planning template on page 52 and work with a teaching partner to create a lesson with the three phases (1) connecting, (2) processing, and (3) transforming and personalizing. Targeting a key strategy over several weeks will lead to increased success for all class members.

Lesson Planning

Lesson: _____

Big Ideas or Key Concepts
Students will understand that . . .

Competencies or Strategies
Students will be able to . . .

Connecting	**Purpose:** Engagement. Activate prior knowledge. Predict content. Focus on a purpose for reading. **I/we will . . .**	How can I/we tap into students' interests, offer appropriate challenges, and increase motivation?
Processing	**Purpose:** Construct meaning. Monitor understanding. Process ideas. **I/we will . . .**	How will I/we help students interact with new ideas they encounter?
Transforming and Personalizing	**Purpose:** Process ideas. Apply knowledge. Reflect on thinking and learning. **I/we will . . .**	How can I/we provide learners with alternatives for demonstrating what they know?

Assessment

If students are engaged and I/we have modeled this well, I/we hope that they will . . .

1.   2.

3.   4.

Pembroke Publishers © 2016 *Student Diversity*, 3rd ed., by Faye Brownlie, Catherine Feniak, Leyton Schnellert ISBN 978-1-55138-318-7

4 Writers Workshop: The Foundation

Our writing program is the unifying factor that links to all that we do in the classroom. It has changed the way we think about planning for teaching, and this has affected the way the students view themselves as learners. It is both powerful and inclusive, as the students' written compositions attest.

In order for students to become skilled writers, they need explicit teaching and lots of time to practise and develop their writing skills. Writers Workshop incorporates writing instruction, extended time for writing, student choice, and student collaboration. The structure of the workshop differentiates for all students as they set personal learning goals while working as part of the classroom community within a whole-class focus. Finally, assessment information is part of the workshop conversation, linking instruction and learning. Students from Kindergarten through secondary school can participate in the Writers Workshop. It begins with a simple idea: everyone has a story to tell. The sharing of these stories helps build a classroom learning community. With these stories as a basis, and the curriculum as a guide, the instructional focus is determined and students develop their skills as authors.

Guiding Principles

We were profoundly influenced by the early work of Donald Graves and his colleagues, such as Nancie Atwell. Initially, Atwell's *In the Middle* helped us set our course. More recently we have been influenced by *Lessons That Change Writers*, also by Atwell.

Atwell (1998) outlined some guiding principles to consider when setting up a Writers Workshop:

- Regular time must be devoted to writing.
- Authors should have the opportunity to choose their own topics.
- Authors need feedback specific to their writing.
- Authors learn the mechanics of writing in the context of their compositions.
- Authors should have time to discuss their writing and read the work of other authors.
- Authors need to read widely.
- Teachers should be knowledgeable about current trends in writing instruction.

Graham et al (2012) have built on this with five recommendations for teaching elementary students to be effective writers:

1. Provide daily time for students to write.

2. Teach students to use the writing process.

3. Teach students to write for a variety of purposes.

4. Teach students to become fluent with handwriting, spelling, sentence construction, typing, and word processing.

5. Create an engaged community of writers.

In *Writing Next: Effective Strategies to Improve Writing of Adolescents in Middle and High Schools,* Graham and Perin (2007) focus on supporting adolescents in becoming effective writers and using writing as a tool for learning. They identify 11 key elements of research-based effective writing:

- writing strategies
- summarization
- working together to plan, draft, revise, and edit
- working with specific, possible goals with each writing piece
- word processing
- sentence combining
- pre-writing
- inquiry to develop ideas and content
- writing process
- studying of writing models
- writing as a way to learn content material

Based on our teaching experiences, we offer several guiding principles of our own:

- Authors benefit from teacher modeling.
- Authors sometimes need specific instruction to foster their writing.
- Writing improves with the development of, not the assignment of, specific criteria.
- Personalized goal setting, planning, and self-assessment can enhance student interest and motivation.
- Teacher feedback during writing in the form of quick conferences that focus on what's working and what's next enhances writing.
- All writers can benefit from, and find success in, a workshop environment.

An Opportunity for Collaborative Teaching

Writing Process Stages
- Pre-writing
- Drafting
- Editing
- Proofreading
- Presenting, sometimes publishing

Writers Workshop works best when an extended period of time (at least 75 minutes beyond Kindergarten, 45 minutes in Kindergarten) is built into the timetable once or twice each week. It is an ideal time for in-class collaborative teaching with the learning resource teacher, although a classroom teacher alone can run Writers Workshop. Together, the classroom teacher and the learning resource teacher determine the needs of the range of students and how best to address these needs. When together in the classroom, the two teachers model, conference, and provide feedback for students individually or in small groups, run editing circles, or teach mini-lessons. During the workshop time, students are involved in the various stages of the writing process: pre-writing, drafting, editing, proofreading, presenting, and sometimes publishing. Sometimes these stages occur with all students simultaneously, sometimes not. Never are these stages considered to be linear.

Lesson Plan Elements

A typical lesson plan for Writers Workshop includes the following activities:

- a mini-lesson taught by the teachers, sometimes as a whole class and sometimes as two smaller groups
- a Status of the Class check to find out the current writing topic of each student
- quiet time for students to write
- individual or small-group conference time with the teachers
- an opportunity to have a short conference with another author
- group sharing time, when authors read a passage from their writing and the rest of the class listens and provides feedback

Writers Workshop as a Foundation in Primary Classrooms

Mentor texts are texts chosen to read with students. These texts often illustrate specific aspects of writing: aspects that we are highlighting with the students.

Writers Workshop is foundational in our classrooms. We strive for all students to see themselves as authors. We see Writers Workshop as a way of connecting both reading and writing with and for our students. We strongly believe that these skills are best taught in a connected and fluid way. By giving students the strategies and tools they need to better self-regulate their learning though a gradual release model of instruction, we see that students are better able to take risks with their learning and stretch themselves further than they had thought possible. We teach mini-lessons that are often connected to a mentor text to offer students tools that they may weave into their writing when the time is right for them. Having a writing folder and the opportunity to share their writing with others helps them to be organized and to have a feeling of ownership for their writing. A two-pocket folder typically has a section for artifacts from mini-lessons and a section for current writing pieces in progress. A Writers Workshop folder is shown below.

A typical folder includes a student's personal word list, a rubric to guide word choice, and drafts of writing in process.

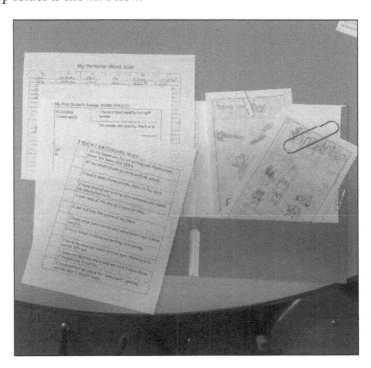

On Friend Write Fridays, students work in partners or trios to write a piece together. They will have chosen something of shared interest. They benefit from generating ideas and texts together.

In their primary classrooms in Yellowknife, Jackie Hawthorn and Kristan Thompson integrate whole-class criteria setting and self-assessment into Writers Workshop to help students increase their confidence and interest in writing. After criteria are created, a copy is placed in the mini-lesson section of their writing folder and in the writing centre. The writing centre is located next to the shelf with students' folders. Key workshop elements in these teachers' classrooms include showing student exemplars, setting up a student writing station and personal writing folders, holding "Friend Write Fridays," coil-binding completed books, and identifying a special spot in the classroom for students' books (see photo). Individual student conferencing is done regularly to assist students in developing their writing skills and in generating ideas and topics for their writing. They welcome fiction and non-fiction writing, but whole-class mini-lessons tend to focus on one of these genres at a time.

A key resource that primary teachers Jackie Hawthorn and Kristan Thompson have found inspiring for implementing Writers Workshop is *About the Authors: Writing Workshop with Our Youngest Writers* by Katie Wood Ray with Lisa B. Cleaveland.

Introducing Writers Workshop to Primary Students

In many primary classes, teachers begin writing in September with a more direct, whole-class lesson that is completed within the 75-minute time frame. Such lessons may include retelling a story that has been read aloud to the class, finding a moment and writing about the moment, or writing the story behind three different pictures. As the students gain the skills to more independently express their thinking on paper, teachers move towards a more open workshop approach, recognizing areas to strengthen in their students' writing and designing responsive lessons.

Here, co-author Catherine Feniak is serving as a learning resource teacher.

What follows is a sequence Catherine worked on with some Grades 2/3 teachers who wanted to introduce Writers Workshop by explicitly teaching leads.

Day 1: Starting with Leads in Grades 2/3

A lead is defined as a sentence that introduces the writing topic and helps to establish the writer's voice. It captures the reader's attention early in the writing.

Prompt the students to examine a variety of leads and discuss what makes them effective. Examples of leads that were used included the following:

- dialogue or a quote: "I can't believe that I once kissed a slug!"
- a bold statement: "If you think that Vancouver is a great place to explore, you need to see Beijing."
- a question: "Have you ever wondered about . . .?"
- a surprising fact: "Although grey whales are enormous mammals their diet is made up of very tiny sea creatures."

Day 2: Building Background Knowledge and Co-constructing Leads

1. Choose three photographs that are connected to an event or a theme to create a conversation between students. As the photo below suggests, our event pertains to an apparent train wreck. You will be displaying the photos, one by one, on the Smart Board.

2. Have students work in A-B partners, matching more verbal students with students who are less verbal. Display the first picture. Students will take turns posing questions to each other about the picture.

3. Invite student pairs to share their most interesting question with the class. Be careful not to provide any clues about the photograph while supporting students in asking questions.

4. Repeat the process with the next two pictures. In response to the second photo, the pairs of students choose their most creative question and after seeing the third photo, their most unusual question, to share with the class. The questions the students share build the knowledge base of the class, deepen their observational skills, and create great curiosity.

See www.whistlerquestion.com/opinion/columnists/setting-the-story-straight-on-whistler-s-train-wreck-1.962088.

5. Provide some historical details about the pictures. Featured here is one of three photos pertaining to an apparent train wreck that occurred in 1956 in Whistler, British Columbia; research later revealed that it was not a train wreck after all.

6. After telling the background story, ask the students to write about what happened based on the photos and the details they have learned.

7. After they finish writing, members of the A-B pairs work together to write a strong lead for a related story, using one of the examples from the previous mini-lesson. Here are some of the leads students wrote about the train:

> Have you ever noticed the Whistler train wreck before? *Jasmine*
> The train wreck looks deadly! *Ryan*
> It was a train that crashed a long time ago. *Hart*
> If you think Vancouver is a cool place, Whistler is much more interesting because at Whistler there was a train that crashed. *Aynsley*

8. After this writing lesson, some of the students may choose to write more about the same topic or event; however, in Writers Workshop the goal is to teach students how to be better writers. These shared writes, led by the teachers and focused on specific aspects of writing, introduce new genres and skills to students as a way to broaden their horizons as authors. Some students take these shared writes and develop them into extended writes. With extended writes, it is usually up to the students to choose what they want to write about.

Day 3: Status of the Class

On the Status of the Class form on page 59, *D* equals "draft."

1. Introduce the Status of the Class routine so that each student author can let the teachers know what he or she is working on during writing time. Model for the students what their choices are:

   - An author who is starting a new composition may say, "Draft 1, new topic."
   - An author who is continuing a composition may say, "Draft 1, island vacation."
   - An author who wants help finding a topic may say, "Conference please."
   - An author who is working on a second draft may say, "Draft 2, Whistler train."

When conferencing, we consider three questions:
1. What is working?
2. What is not?
3. What is next?
As the sample "Conferences Notes" form on page 60 records, Hannah was excited about the mango and ice-cream in her writing. To add more detail and make a greater personal connection, she and a teacher talked about how to add in a recipe for a mango smoothie — a prompt that grew from questions #2 and #3, led by Hannah and polished by the teacher.

2. Circulate among the students with a copy of the Status of the Class form and find out each student's current writing topic. Do not have all the students wait to write while their peers are learning to describe their status. When co-teaching in a writing class, teachers are well able to coach and provide feedback to each student, to be aware of how much writing is being completed by each student, and to monitor how long it takes each student to finish a composition.

3. Once the writing topics are established, continue to circulate throughout the class to have short conferences and provide feedback to each student. Notice what is working for the writer and extend the thinking by asking a question or providing a prompt. The conference focus could include the story lead, detail, organization, the ending, or topics related to recent mini-lessons, but it is always focused on meaning first — not on conventions, spelling, or grammar.

Status of the Class

Names	October 1	October 8	October 15	
Daniel	D1 new	D1 comic	D1 accomplishment	
James	D1 Toronto	D1 Halloween	D2 Toronto	
Leila	D1 horseback riding	D1 story scared about birthdays	D2 special place	
Kara	D1 England	D1 continued	D2 England	
Griffin	D1 story quest	D1 comic Conference	Proofreading Hawaii	
Sienna	D1 horseback riding	D1 continued	D1 special place Indonesia	
Theo	D1 castle story	D1 spy story. Lead with a quote	Good copy Australian beach story	
David	D1 cyber chicken	D1 Ooba (lead)	D1 special place	
Hannah	D1 fav. food	D1 Halloween	D2 fav. food	

4. Take notes weekly as a reminder of each student's focus. Record what is noticed about the writing both in terms of the author's strengths and areas for growth.

Day 4: Learning How to Edit

Editing, or learning how to return to your work and revisit it with new eyes, requires explicit teaching. It is not an automatic process for most student writers.

1. Outline for the students several ways to edit writing, for example, adding, changing, or deleting words or ideas and rearranging text by moving it around.

2. Use the Smart Board or document camera to display a draft of a story you have written, a story that includes some of the aspects of writing that you are developing with your students. Have students read the story, and notice what you have done well. Ask for ideas about how to improve. Mark up the writing with their ideas. Highlight or star specific aspects of the writing that work well. Use the caret symbol for additions, arrows to indicate where text could be moved to, and numbers to show where longer additions of text could go.

3. Explain that when students are ready to revise their compositions, they are moving from a first draft to a second draft to perhaps a third draft. This is what writers do to improve their writing.

Daniel	James	Leila	Kara	Griffin
Draft 2, My Accomplishment. Revising to add details about his bike and how he felt as he rode for the first time. How he protected himself from falling although he was a good rider even when he first rode.		*Draft 2, Special Place. Revising her lead to explain that visitors to her special place need to solve a riddle!*		
Sienna	Theo	David	Hannah	Jacob
Draft 2, Trip to Indonesia. Adding details about seeing wild monkeys and collecting miniature sand dollars. Discussed her closing sentence.			*Draft 1, Favorite food — mango and ice-cream. Discussed adding a recipe for a mango smoothie into her writing.*	
Osmond	Alvin	Austin	JJ	Joy
Draft 1, Special Place. Revising to include details about a hot day in Hawaii and wanting a cooling smoothie. We talked about changing the pronoun "you" to "I" when he's writing about himself.	*Draft 2, Special Place, Sydney, Australia. Very elaborate sketch of the Sydney Harbour area. Revising his writing by adding details he included in his drawing.*	*Draft 1, Beach in Hawaii (special place). We talked about how he could add his feelings about the beach to show the audience why it's a special place.*		
Taryn	Tom	Abdisa	Laila	Audrey
	*Draft 1, His Accomplishment = diving. Adding in details about the kinds of belly flops and cannon ball jumps that he made. I started with short notes of our chat and he continued with points that he wanted to include. *show these notes to class tomorrow.*		*Draft 1, Her Accomplishment. Used a question for a lead. Talked about showing, not telling to describe her fear. Used lots of repetition of the word accomplishment.*	*Draft 1, Piano Exam Accomplishment. Talked about how she could show her nervousness before her piano exam (cold, clammy hands etc).*
Roman	Elizabeth			
Draft 1, Special Place, Honolulu. Revising as he writes.	*Draft 1, Special Place – her bedroom. Adding how she feels when she's in her bedroom/Why it's special to her.*			

Notes: Show Tom's notes to himself as an example of revising.

Getting Intermediate, Middle, and Secondary Students Started

At other times of the year, prompts could include special places, celebrations, topics such as respect or kindness, and content such as the impact of geography on community.

On the first day of Writers Workshop, the goal is to get each student writing about a personal experience. A typical September prompt is to ask students to visualize some of the places, people, things, and events that they experienced over the summer holiday. We model each part of the process for the students, then invite them to follow our process and borrow any of our ideas to spark their thinking.

Pre-writing 1: Finding a Topic

1. In a way that is visible to the students, the teacher records three everyday topics that she could use for writing, perhaps Grandma, amber, and kayaking.

2. Students think of three topics they could write about and record them on paper.

3. Students ask questions of the teacher about her topics. The teacher encourages the kinds of questions that help students make connections, add details, and use expressive language. (For example, the teacher might say: "When you ask me about my interest in amber, I can instantly imagine when I first learned the story of how amber is found in the sea.")

4. Students share their three topics with a partner and together engage in the same questioning process.

Pre-writing 2: Going Deeper with the Topic

1. The teacher models recording a web of ideas for any or all of her three topics, based on her thinking after the questioning.

2. Each student begins to record a web of ideas for any or all of their three topics. Students can show their thinking in a web using drawings and words. (Doing this is especially helpful for ELL students.)

3. From their webs, students each choose one topic to write about.

4. Partners interview each other using open-ended questions as prompts to discuss ideas not yet included in the web.

5. Final details are added to the web after this interview.

Drafting the Story

1. As students are ready, they move from their web to writing a first draft of a story. The teachers also write.

2. After a few minutes of writing, the teachers move through the room to provide formative feedback to each student. They read over the writer's shoulder and comment on something positive — what's working. They also ask a question or provide a prompt to support the writer in figuring out what's next. As students become more self-regulated, they request a

conference and bring specific queries about their draft that they want to address with one of the teachers.

3. Students write for 15 to 20 minutes.

Sharing and Exploring Leads

1. Each writer in the class, including the teacher(s), reads aloud his or her first sentence: the lead. (Alternatively, a chosen focus might be powerful words or language that creates an image or touches the heart.)

2. The class identifies what catches their attention or what works in the leads. Frequently, students will notice that effective leads are humorous, use dialogue, or use action to gain attention.

3. These ideas are recorded. They will be used in a later mini-lesson on leads.

4. The teacher reinforces how much the students already know about leads. This has been the first mini-lesson.

Editing and Building a Skill Focus

On Day 2 of Writers Workshop, the class of intermediate, middle, or secondary school students moves more deeply into editing and work on leads. The two teachers determine their respective roles based on their personal background and expertise. It is a fluid process.

1. One of the teachers reads several effective leads from novels or short stories.

2. Students form heterogeneous groups chosen by the teachers. One copy of a paragraph from a teacher's writing is provided for each group to read. Here is an authentic sample.

> This summer, I learned that teamwork and a tidal chart are very important when paddling a kayak. A friend and I decided to rent a double kayak for an afternoon outing. We set out with all the essential equipment except for a chart of the changing ocean tides, which had been left in the car. We paddled into a narrow channel. Suddenly we were traveling backwards even though we were paddling forwards. As I looked at the water churning around us I realized that we were paddling against the surging tide. *We've got to paddle harder*, I thought to myself.

3. Together, each group discusses and rewrites the lead in the teacher's story using humor, action, or dialogue so that it will capture the reader's attention.

4. Based on this discussion, students write two or three different leads for their stories.

Silence Is Productive

Many students recognize that they do their best writing in a quiet classroom with few interruptions. In one of our classes, the students took turns at the beginning of the Writers Workshop to teach the word *silence* in their first language. A Spanish-speaking boy from Mexico proudly taught the word *silencio* to his classmates and wrote the word on the board. The next day a Mandarin-speaking student introduced the Chinese character for silence.

5. Each student shares leads with a partner and together they determine how effective the leads are and why they are effective.

6 Students choose the most effective lead of their personal experience stories from Day 1 to engage their audience through humor, action, or dialogue.

Discussing, Conferencing, and Drafting

Following the first few Writers Workshop classes, the students and teachers discuss what is working well in the workshop. The students brainstorm what the class expectations are in order to make the Writers Workshop a productive time for all authors.

A second area for discussion explores the kinds of questions that an author might ask during a conference with the teacher. Once a first draft of the personal experience story is finished, students can request a conference with one of the teachers to gain more feedback on their writing. Since conferences are designed to be short meetings between an author and a teacher, the student comes prepared to ask the teacher a question specific to the writing. In a mini-lesson at the beginning of the year, students learn that a typical conference is about five minutes long.

A third discussion area is what students can do if they cannot think of a new writing topic. We often have students generate a running list of meaningful moments and experiences from their lives; for examples, see Georgia Heard's *heart maps*, as described in *Awakening the Heart*, and Nancie Atwell's *writing territories*, which are outlined in *Lessons That Change Writers*. Students can add to and select from this list at any time.

In a conference, teachers will not have a chance to read an entire draft unless it is a short piece. Based on the editing and skill focus lessons, students will choose conference topics such as these:

- lead
- use of dialogue
- development of the plot
- ending of the story
- effective imagery
- use of language
- paragraph structure; when to begin and end

Determining the Status of the Class

Following a mini-lesson, one of the teachers records the date and topic of the composition that each of the authors is currently writing. The Status of the Class check is completed quickly so that the students can settle into their writing tasks. When a student's name is called, the topic being written about and the draft number (for example, D1 or D2) is provided for the teacher to record. The teacher also records if students ask for a conference during the Status of the Class check so that a conference can be scheduled during the writing period.

Using the Status of the Class chart, teachers can quickly monitor the writing being produced by each author. If a student is on the first draft of a topic for a long time, one of the teachers will have a conference with the student to discuss the author's plan for ending the story. A conference is also needed for a student who keeps changing topics without completing a final draft. Students have the option to put aside a draft before it is completed; however, it is important for authors to experience the writing process by revising and editing their work. When students are guided through the writing process, they learn how to strengthen their writing and experience the pride of completing a composition. Providing teacher support to monitor each student's progress is central to success in Writers Workshop.

During a Status of the Class check, a student response "Draft 1, holiday" would indicate that it is the first time the student has written a story about a holiday; a few days later, the same student might say, "Draft 3, holiday" to indicate that two revisions have been made to the initial draft.

Status of the Class Chart

	Oct. 3	Oct. 10	Oct. 15	Oct. 17	Nov. 1	Nov. 14	Nov. 17	Nov. 21	Nov. 24	Nov. 28
Kamal-preet	D1 fly	D2✓ © lost	©✓	comp. lost	D1 poem	D1 poem	D1 © →parody	D2 parody	D2 →comp.	D2 lib comp.
Gurjit	D1 lost →	©✓	D1 lost →	→	LRT	D1 lost	→cont'd	D1 comic	→D1 cont'd	parody D2
Andrew	D1 skiing →	→	D1	D2 comp.		D1 comic	→D1 cont'd	D1 cont'd →	→	→D1
Jessica	D1 Florida →	→	D1 comp.	→		D2 comp.	D2	D2 →	D2 Florida comp.	D1 © L.A.
Steven	D1 lost dog →	©✓		D2 comp. B-Jay		D2 comp.	D1 comic	D1 cont'd	D2 comp.	D2 comp.

D = draft
© = conference requested
New = new composition has been started; no topic yet
LRT = learning resource teacher assisting student
comp. = on computer

The Group Share

P Praise
Q Questions
S Suggestions

A mini-lesson at the beginning of the year introduces the Group Share process to intermediate, middle, and secondary students. Some teachers choose to offer an opportunity for students to share their writing at any time during the workshop whereas others have designated sharing times. The Group Share can be physically organized as a sharing circle. All students bring a chair to form the circle; this format reinforces that every voice, every perspective, and every student is equally valued.

All students are expected to take part in the Group Share by actively listening to their peers. The students who want feedback on their writing read a portion of their work aloud. Students in the audience are taught to respond to the author by offering Praise, Questions, and Suggestions (PQS) pertinent to the written passage. The responses must be specific to the writing so that the feedback is useful to the author; for example, a student who offers praise by saying she liked the composition because it was funny is asked to identify the specific parts of the passage that were funny.

Using their own writing, the teachers initially model the kinds of praise, questions, and suggestions that can be made, so that the students learn how to offer feedback in a respectful and positive manner. Initially, some students may prefer to participate in the Group Share by asking one of the teachers to read their writing anonymously. Once students are familiar with this process, more of them are keen to participate by reading aloud their own writing and by offering praise, questions, and suggestions.

Having a teacher record the feedback allows the author to really listen to classmates without trying to remember all that is being said and gives the author a written record of the classmates' feedback. It also places high value on the feedback and models another use of writing.

In some intermediate classes, over the course of a term, all students are expected to read their writing for a PQS session with the entire class. As the student leads the session, the classroom teacher records the feedback. When the final suggestion is given, the teacher reads back the notes so the class can edit them, ensuring that the record is accurate. The notes are then given to the author to use as he or she sees fit during revisions. When students internalize how to work well with PQS, they can meet in editing groups of four to follow the same process — one author reading, one recording, and the other two providing feedback.

In middle school and secondary classrooms, Writers Workshop provides an important opportunity for teachers to build relationships with their students. Teachers get to know students through the experiences they choose to write about and the manner in which they tell their stories. Through repeated modeling, first by teachers and then by students, as well as opportunities for sharing, student authors begin to take risks in sharing their personal experiences. By the modeling of positive feedback, a classroom community is built, based on values of trust and respect for individuality.

Mini-lesson: Free Verse Poetry

Free verse poetry is accessible to students of all ages. The format highlights detail and description without the constraint of sentences. As such, it also supports the language and learning of diverse learners.

Introducing different genres of writing during mini-lessons provides authors with new ideas for writing and expands their repertoire of ways to express their thinking. Free verse poetry is one of the mini-lessons that we teach early in the school year, since it allows students to express their ideas in an open-ended format and often appeals to writers who are challenged to write. We believe that all students can learn to write and can enjoy writing. Lessons such as this help convince students to believe in themselves.

The following mini-lesson is based on students taking a guided walk outside to observe seasonal changes. Students transform their observations of nature into descriptive phrases that shape a free verse poem. Here are the steps we follow:

1. Distribute hand-held magnifiers to pairs of students.

Students can record observations as descriptive phrases, words, drawings with labels, or drawings with labels and phrases explaining them. Younger students can simply record their observations, and these can be categorized once back in the classroom.

2. Give each student a chart, such as the one begun below, for observing and recording descriptive details using the senses. Ask students to record as much information as they can on the chart.

Autumn Observation Sheet

Sights	Sounds	Smells	Touch	Scientific Data	Other

3. Students walk outside, talk, and record their observations in small groups.

4. After returning to the classroom, students share a phrase or description from their observation sheets with the class.

5. Recording each idea on the Smart Board, the teacher builds a class list of observations.

6. Using the class list, the teacher works with the students to determine which descriptions to include in their free verse poem.

7. Groups of students work together to make decisions about how to order the descriptive phrases for a free verse poem.

8. The finished poems are read aloud by each group.

9. Students share what they noticed about the order of the images in these poems.

10. Students then write their own poems, building and borrowing from the class and small-group work.

Mini-lessons that introduce poetic conventions such as simile, metaphor, imagery, and repetition can be taught to help strengthen the skills of developing poets in the elementary, middle, and secondary grades.

Amanda and Lewis provide powerful autumn examples from this experience. Charanpreet also provides a powerful example, focusing on one object that he has seen on his walk. These three students represent the diversity within the classroom.

Autumn

Trees are surprisingly vibrant with shades of red and yellow.
The cool tingling breeze is crisp and fresh.
A light fragrance of dew is in the morning air.
It is autumn.
Leaves gently twirling around to the brown and yellow floor.
The days are short and cool.
Birds are flying south in their orderly fashion.
Trees sway as the wind blows them swiftly.
It is autumn.
I see it.
I smell it.
I hear it.
I feel it.
It is autumn.

Amanda

Fall

As the leaves fall gracefully to the ground like a ship slowing sinking to the misty ocean floor,
I find that I am one step closer to, but also further away from the summer that once was.
As the relaxing fall breeze flows through the street like a silent army preparing for battle,
I see the black clouds having all the power of the god called nature.
As the rain starts to slowly fall to the ground like a leaking faucet,
The streets turn to a slippery marsh of leaves.
As the murky water flows to the storm drains,
I taste the first flake of snow as it touches my tongue when this season passes once again . . .

Lewis

Rock

Staying still like silicon
Little shiny dots like a million pieces of broken mirror
Hard like a piece of steel
Has no home
Has a life who knows?
Sharp like a knife.
Charanpreet

Mini-lesson: Letting Pictures Tell the Story

When students struggle to write a narrative story, we introduce Letting Pictures Tell the Story, one of our favorite strategies to motivate writing. This strategy is designed for use with a whole class, small groups, or individual students.

1. Ask students to fold a piece of paper into six sections.

2. Choose six words that will have emotional appeal to the students or words that have curricular connections to a unit of study: for example, *escape, hidden, determination, hope, separation, equality.*

3. Say the first word aloud, and for one minute have students draw all the images and connected ideas they can in the first section of their paper.

4. Repeat this process until all six words have been illustrated.

5. With some, but not after every word, encourage students to share their thinking and drawing with partners, and hear the range of interpretations in the class.

6. Ask students to think about the connections between the words or illustrations and to choose at least four of them to include in a story.

Letting Pictures Tell the Story is an effective mini-lesson to develop narrative. It begins with student sketches and fosters plenty of talk. The mini-lesson is intended for intermediate, middle, and secondary school students.

Review with students that, in addition to the four words, the story should include characters, conflict, a climax, and a resolution.

An ELL student conveys understanding of the concepts of escape, hope, equality, separation, hidden, and determination through simple stick figures.

Tiffany, a Grade 7 writer, has developed a strong voice in her writing as she includes the four words *hope*, *escape*, *equality*, and *determination*.

The Vow

It just isn't fair. Nothing's fair, Martin thought sullenly, sitting in detention. *Just because I wrote an essay he didn't like. I get detention?* He looked around the room in vain for <u>hope</u> of <u>escape</u>. It was a warm and sunny day, a perfect day to be outside. A teacher, Mr. McKeal, walked in, interrupting his thoughts.

"Hello, Martin. Now what did you do today?"

"Nothing," Martin said defensively. "We were all supposed to write an essay about what we think is important in life, and then read it out loud to the whole class. I wrote about <u>equality</u>, and after I read it out loud, Mr. Green started making stupid suggestions. I got angry and said something, so he sent me here."

Mr. McKeal raised his eyebrows. "Oh, really? Mr. Green said you wrote something inappropriate, and he was just trying to help you. Then you started yelling at him."

Martin started to protest, but was cut off by a gesture by Mr. McKeal's hand. "The way I see it, you were being inexcusably rude to your teacher. Although Mr. Green may not have been able to share your point of view, you should have held back your anger. As your punishment, you will write a hundred word essay to apologize to your teacher. Next time, I'd suggest you write something your teacher agrees on. Okay?" When Martin nodded, Mr. McKeal dismissed him.

Frustrated, Martin ran out of the school. *Nobody understands. They're all too narrow-minded.* Taking a deep breath of the fresh autumn air, he made up his mind. Blazing with <u>determination</u>, he made a silent vow. *One day,* he thought, *one day I'll write an essay about what I believe in that they will never, ever forget.*

Mini-lesson: Power Paragraphs for Information Writing

Throughout their schooling, students are required to write information paragraphs in order to demonstrate an understanding. We find that knowing this formula for a power paragraph sets the stage for each student to be successful. Needless to say, once the formula is understood and controlled, the student personalizes it and moves beyond the formula.

Early in the school year we teach students how to communicate ideas and information using the power paragraph format. The Power Paragraph graphic organizer (page 74) is designed to help students choose a main idea, include relevant facts and supporting details, and write them in a logical order. We start with one paragraph and, as the students' proficiency grows, we add more paragraphs to expand on the topic. Before long, the students are able to write short essays to communicate their ideas about a topic. Although this may seem to be formulaic writing, we believe that if students first gain control with the structure of this kind of writing, they can quickly internalize it and move beyond the graphic organizer. It is a starting point that supports those students who are challenged by the brevity of a summary and supports those students who are challenged by how to organize an informative paragraph. Some teachers begin teaching this structure with topics familiar to the students, such as pets or hockey, then move to writing connected to reading, as in the following example.

The Power Paragraph organizer appears as a line master for students at the end of this chapter.

1. Students receive a copy of the Power Paragraph graphic organizer.

2. Students are given a copy of a compelling article and directed to read it on their own or with support, as needed.

3. Working in pairs, students discuss what struck them about the article; for example, it might be something that surprised them, something they learned, or something they would like to know more about.

4. Students then work as a class to choose one fact or big idea in the article. This is recorded in point form on the graphic organizer on the Smart Board.

5. Students, as a class, reread the article to find two details that support or tell more about the fact or big idea. These are added in point form to the graphic organizer.

6. Students continue working in pairs to identify the second fact and supporting details; they record this information on the graphic organizer.

7. Students continue the process to identify and record a third fact with supporting details.

8. Students move into small groups to review the three facts and supporting details. They work together to construct a topic sentence that introduces the topic of the paragraph in an interesting way.

9. Each group shares their topic sentence so the class can determine which of the sentences is the most effective.

10. Working with a partner, students weave the ideas in the first fact and the supporting details into one or two complete sentences, using connecting words such as *and*, *but*, *so*, *because*, and *therefore*.

11. Students repeat this process until the facts and details have all been rewritten into complete sentences.

12. The topic sentence is reread and edited, if needed, to fit the rest of the sentences in the paragraph.

13. Each student makes decisions as to the order in which the sentences are best presented.

14. Starting with the topic sentence, the entire paragraph is written. It can now be edited or proofread, as required.

From Writers Workshop to Inquiry

Don Blazevich finds that incorporating Writers Workshop with his Grades 2/3 students allows him to honor everyone in a collaborative community of writers. Explicit instruction becomes responsive to student needs and allows time for practice and repeated visiting of a variety of skills that are applied directly to the craft of writing. Don has expanded the Writers Workshop emphasis on choice into the realm of inquiry, further extending his students' role as active participants in their own learning. He uses conversation and curiosity to invite students into asking questions that are important to them and to co-construct curriculum understandings together.

A Five-Step Process

Don identified five steps to the inquiry cycle for his primary students. He introduced the steps and matched each step with a finger on one of his hands. The steps are as follows:

1. Ask a question.

2. Become curious. Ask more questions!

3. Find answers to your questions.

4. Make a web. Use your own words.

5. Share your learning.

Modelling the Inquiry Process

1. Ask a question: What is water?
In the curriculum for Grade 2, the theme of Water is prevalent in Science. Don decided to ask an open-ended question — *What is water?* — and let his students take the lead.

2. Become curious: Ask more questions!
From that single question written for all to see, Don prompted his students to ask any question about water that they would like to know the answer to. The only requirement was that everyone had to have a question. Helping others come up with a question was encouraged within the community of thinkers. To Don's pleasant surprise, the class accumulated 34 questions!

3. Find answers to your questions.
Now came the challenging part: finding answers to the questions. Don enlisted the aid of the school's librarian and asked her to pull all the "water" books in the school library: the goal was to create a text set. He also told the students to ask their families to help them find answers to their questions. As part of the daily routine, Don read aloud with the students from these library books signed out from the library during Science time, which was now referred to as "Water Inquiry." The children delighted in finding answers to many of the questions and gleefully pointed to the questions they had discovered answers to. Don's students always had access to the library books on water. Occasionally, students would claim, "I knew that already."

4. Make a web. Use your own words.
During Water Inquiry time, when students learned answers or interesting information about water, Don would ask the students to tell him the most important word, or words, from the book or passage. He added these "key words" to a class web. Students also added to their webs.

Don then asked, "What are you learning about your questions?" In this process, he found that students would often share short statements of fact. Through modeling, they began to look at how scientists, and the books they were reading, would share information. They practised expressing what they were learning using long, interesting sentences to help them sound like a scientist. This frequent verbal rehearsal provided repeated practice in creating interesting sentences as well as confirming information that was being processed.

Where possible, Don photocopied one page that contained at least part of the answer to each question. Individually, or with a partner, the students circled key words they felt were important to use in answering their question. Don modeled this process with one of the questions.

At the end of each Water Inquiry block, Don asked students to identify which inquiry questions they had answered. Students could choose any question from Step 2 for which they would like to share the answer.

5. *Share your learning.*

Don would ask the students, using only their webs as a scaffold, to tell him why they chose their key words. They practised answering their questions as scientists. Each question was recorded on a paper shaped like a raindrop, and students recorded their answer on the raindrop. Extra copies of each raindrop were available for the students as many students wanted to answer other students' questions. As they answered questions, they added their raindrops to their "inquiry cloud." Motivation remained high as many students wanted to collect every classmate's raindrop.

In the end, there was a virtual Water Inquiry rainstorm in the classroom.

Critical Literacy in Writers Workshop

In Belinda Chi's Grades 4 and 5 class, they have been exploring critical literacy by reading fairytales. Belinda takes her students through several different stories to discuss characters, elements of a fairytale, and how characters compare to people in the real world. Throughout these lessons, she asks students what they notice and encourages them to think deeply about the underlying messages presented to readers through fairytales. She teaches her students to be critical thinkers, as readers and as writers, as they prepare to write their own stories in Writers Workshop.

Day 1: Thinking about Character — Good versus Evil

Belinda's Grades 4 and 5 students sit at the carpet for the read-aloud. Today, they are reading *Sleeping Beauty*, a classic fairytale. Before reading, Belinda reminds students to think about the characters in the story, as they will be discussing them at the end of the story. Here is how you might adopt her approach.

1. After reading, ask students to identify the main characters in the story.

2. Record the names of the main characters on the board — one "good" character and one "evil" character.

3. Have students brainstorm facts they know about each of the characters. Together as a class, build a web.

4. Ask students to think about three statements that are true to each of the characters. For example:

> Sleeping Beauty would share her snacks.
> Sleeping Beauty would help an animal that was hurt.
> Sleeping Beauty would play with us at recess.

> The Evil Queen would share only poisonous snacks.
> The Evil Queen would not help someone in need.
> The Evil Queen would keep us apart from our friends.

5. Once students feel confident about the differences between good characters and evil characters, they return to their desks and turn to their Writers

Workshop binders to brainstorm good and evil characters to use in their own stories, later on. It is important for students to understand their characters well, in order to write stories that are true to the characters they create.

Day 2: Exploring the Elements of a Fairytale

Common Fairytale Features

The story always begins with "Once upon a time . . ."
It ends with "Happily ever after."
The story is usually about love.
The good characters are usually a princess and a prince.
There are evil characters.
The princess and prince don't know each other's names.
Prince with no name saves the princess.
Princess is always beautiful and in danger.
Father is clueless.
Birth mother dies, and stepmother is always evil.

The teacher might pair the question about why princesses are usually slim with an appropriate picture book image or photograph.

On Day 2, Belinda and the children sit at the carpet again for another read-aloud. This time the title Belinda is sharing is *Snow White and the Seven Dwarfs*. Before reading, she asks the students to think about the similarities between the last fairytale they read, *Sleeping Beauty*, and this one they are about to hear.

1. After the read-aloud, ask students what similarities they notice about this fairytale and the previous read-aloud.

2. Record student thinking on the board.

3. Take one of the statements about fairytale features, and with the students, examine it closely. For instance, take this "typical" representation of a princess:

   Princess is always beautiful and in danger.

   Be sure to model questions, such as "Why are the princesses usually slim?" Students share questions such as the following around the statement.

   - Why are they always described as beautiful?
   - Why are the princesses usually light skinned?
   - Why are they always rich?
   - How come they always have to be saved by a prince, whose name they don't know?
   - Why can't she save herself?

Insights Students Have Shared

"I think the princess can be strong — remember the Paper Bag Princess."
"It's not smart to just let someone kiss you."
"Why can't they just save each other?"
"You do not have to be skinny to be a princess."

4. Pose probing questions to the students to explore their thinking:

   - Does this mean that all princesses have to be slim and light skinned to be beautiful?
   - Since the princess has to be saved by a prince, does this mean that girls are weak?
   - Is it safe to let a stranger save you with a kiss?

   This kind of questioning prompts students to think about the elements of a fairytale and how these characters are not representative of real people. Students are now beginning to think critically about these stories and to use a critical lens to deepen their understanding as readers and writers. Jot students' ideas down and acknowledge their deep thinking and ability to identify hidden messages.

5. Invite students to return to their Writers Workshop folders and on their own brainstorm questions about the characters in their stories.

Day 3: Comparing Characters in Fairytales to People in the Real World

In the first two lessons, students would have thought deeply about the characters in two stories and what they had noticed about fairytales. They now reflect on the differences between fairytales and the real world they live in. Today, one student has brought in *Cinderella* for Belinda to read to the class. The students gather at the carpet, ready to participate as critical thinkers.

Questions Students Have Asked

- Why does Cinderella's mother die?
- Why is the stepmother evil?
- How come Cinderella's father doesn't know what's going on?
- How come Cinderella and the Prince don't know each other's names?
- Don't other people have the same size feet as Cinderella?
- Why does "happily ever after" always mean the boy and girl getting married?

1. Throughout the story, students raise their hands and await their turn to share their thinking, asking questions.

2. After reading the story aloud, take one of the questions and unpack it further. What does it mean? What does it represent? What is it trying to tell the readers?

   Why does "happily ever after" always mean the boy and girl getting married?

   Probe the students' thinking by asking questions like these:

   - Does being happy mean you have to be married?
   - Does love have to be between a boy and a girl?
   - What happens after they get married?
   - Does getting married mean that there are no other problems?
   - What does happiness mean to you?

   Students respond as critical thinkers and participate in the teacher-facilitated discussion.

3. After the discussion, ask the students to return to their desks and their Writers Workshop folders. Invite the students to write a reflection on this question: *What does "happily ever after" mean to you?*

   To help further students' thinking about their own story writing, you might provide another reflection activity through this question: *What makes a good ending to a story?*

4. Students use these writing activities to critically think about how they want to shape their own stories, their own characters, and their own endings.

Teachers can facilitate a conversation with students related to their responses, create criteria from the responses, and encourage students to refer to these criteria when writing their stories and responding to each other's stories.

Becoming Prepared to Write

Critical literacy is an important skill for students as readers and writers to develop. It helps them to deepen their understanding and ask thoughtful questions about their texts. Through lessons and activities such as those presented here, students are helped to feel prepared before delving into writing their own stories. The critical literacy they are developing will allow them to be more purposeful authors; they understand their characters more clearly and can anticipate what kind of message they want to leave with their readers.

A Powerful Approach

Writers Workshop is a foundational approach in our classrooms. It nurtures students as authors. It gives them voice and choice. Students learn to self-regulate their learning. Writers Workshop also opens up space for teachers to conference with students, personalizing learning. It integrates beautifully with other powerful approaches such as reading workshop, literacy centres and stations, critical literacy, inquiry, information and literature circles, and culturally responsive teaching. Everyone is welcome in this community of authors.

Power Paragraph

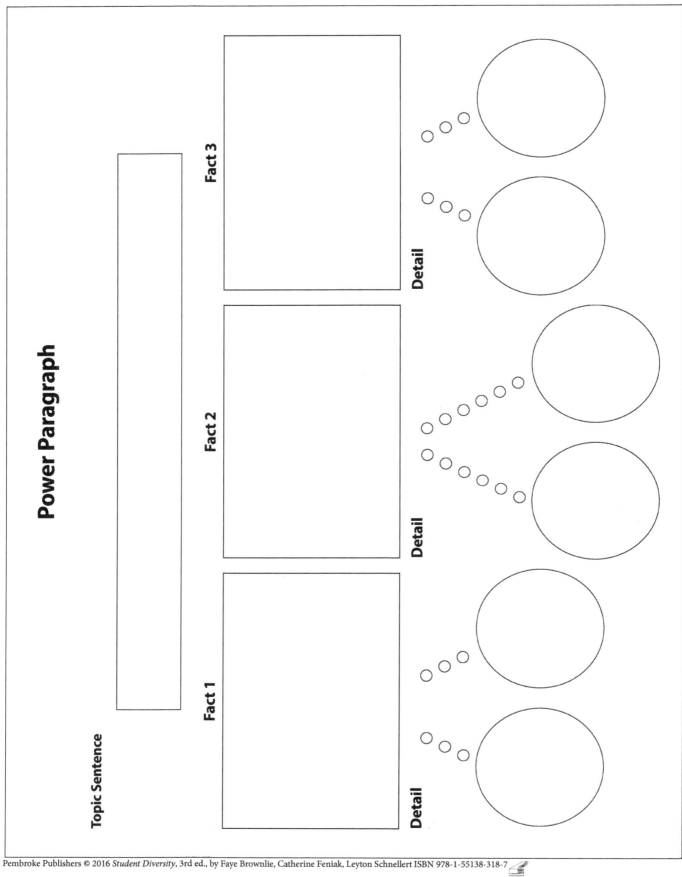

Topic Sentence

Fact 1

Fact 2

Fact 3

Detail

Detail

Detail

Pembroke Publishers © 2016 *Student Diversity*, 3rd ed., by Faye Brownlie, Catherine Feniak, Leyton Schnellert ISBN 978-1-55138-318-7

5 Introducing Narrative Writing

We champion the importance of teacher collaboration. We are passionate in our belief that students learn better in classroom communities where they feel they belong. We believe that all students can be and should be included in ways that improve the learning of all students. We believe that writing is the foundation from which our classrooms grow as learning communities.

Two collaborative scenarios for narrative writing follow: the first involving a classroom teacher and a learning resource teacher in a Kindergarten class, the other involving four classroom teachers and one learning resource teacher in three classes that combine Grades 6 and 7 students.

Working Together: Writing in Kindergarten

The beginning of a new school year is an optimal time for learning resource teachers who work with students who are learning English and students with challenges to co-teach with Kindergarten teachers. Learning resource teachers can support the emergent literacy skills of the children and assist in determining each learner's strengths and learning needs. The first few months of Kindergarten are a key period during which a second teacher can help the children in making a successful transition from home to school and can develop relationships with each child. It is also a key time for the teachers to work together to learn about each child's facility with language, to establish the routines of the classroom, to support the children during activities, and to observe them as they learn. Collaborative planning and instruction in Writers Workshop is a way to achieve these goals and to support the emergent literacy skills of all students. All children have stories to tell. Writers Workshop helps us find and develop these stories.

Because of our belief in the power of creating learning communities and of Writers Workshop, we uncover children's interests through discussion, through observing the books each child chooses, through artwork, and through field trips. We build on these interests with our book selection and hands-on displays. These lead to further inquiry throughout the year through oral language, movement, writing, reading, and drawing — all key components of Writers Workshop for early learners.

In Cindy Lee's Kindergarten class, 40 percent of the students were English language learners and 35 percent of the students were Aboriginal. In addition, 2 of the 19 children were designated as having special educational needs that were detailed in individual education plans. Catherine was the learning resource teacher. They began September working together in the classroom, an hour a day, in this five-day sequence.

Catherine Feniak, the learning resource teacher who outlines the Kindergarten-level collaboration, is also one of the authors of this resource.

Day 1: Drawing the Family

1. As a learning resource teacher, I modeled quick sketches of the members of my family. While drawing, I *thought aloud* as I included details about each member of my family. For example, I said: "I wear blue glasses and have dark, short hair. Today I am wearing a yellow shirt with green stripes and black pants." As I noted this, I added these details, using crayons to color the drawing.

2. I intentionally drew a tiny person whom I described as my mom. I asked if the drawing was clear and easily seen. The children replied that they could not see the drawing of my mom very well. So I reminded myself aloud to draw my pictures big enough for the audience to see clearly and redrew my mom while the children gave feedback on the size, details, and colors used in the drawing.

3. Finally, I added my name below the drawing of myself.

4. Cindy showed word cards with corresponding pictures or drawings to label family members: Mom, Dad, Sister, Brother, Grandma, Grandpa, Aunt, and Uncle. We added extended family since many of our students live with members of their extended family. Children then matched these word cards to my drawing. The word cards began our word wall.

5. We paired the children as A-B partners (students sit *knee to knee and eye to eye*). The classroom teacher and I modeled how partner A talks about her family while partner B listens, and then vice versa. Next, the children tried the activity. Partner A listened as partner B described the people in his or her family. We moved around to help the children learn the turn-taking format. After several minutes, the partners reversed roles. Whenever possible, we partnered children who were in the early stages of learning English with someone who spoke the same first language but had more proficiency. Speaking the first language helps the child learning English to express ideas, ask questions, and make connections between the two languages. We also encouraged children to bring family pictures to school to use in talking to one another.

6. We reviewed the criteria established with my drawing (draw big enough for the audience to see, use lots of color, and add details). In several weeks, the criteria for drawing would simply become "Big, bright, and bold" (Reid and Schultze with Petersen 2012).

7. The children moved to their workspaces to draw their family following the co-created criteria. We used coil-bound books of legal-sized paper without lines as the notebooks.

8. We circulated as the children drew. We had short conferences with each child to hear how the child described his or her drawing. We reinforced the criteria for drawing and writing. For example, we might say: "I see that you have included each member of your family using big, clear drawings. You've included great details like your dad's black beard. Did you include lots of color and details to show me what each person is wearing?" Comments like these provided each child with feedback about what worked in the drawing as well as where there was an area for improvement. We also wrote a simple question about the drawing, based on what we had learned about the child,

such as "What does your family like to do together?" We read the question to the child, then invited the child to answer. We reread the question together using paired reading techniques and tracked the print with our fingers. Each sample was date-stamped.

Day 2: Sharing What the Family Likes to Do

1. We wrote each child's name on a craft stick and then each time student input was desired, we drew a craft stick. The children enjoyed the randomness of the draw and the fact that each classmate had one turn before anyone had a second turn. Some children also liked to return to the jar of craft sticks to find their names and those of others.

2. We read aloud two picture books that highlighted the diversity of families: *Families, Families, Families* by Suzanne Lang, illustrated by Max Lang; and *Families* by Shelly Rotner and Shelia M. Kelly. Using the craft sticks, students were invited to make a connection to the stories during the reading.

"Big, bright, and bold," the criteria for drawing, derives from *What's Next for This Beginning Writer?* by Janine Reid and Betty Schultze, with Ulla Petersen. The revised edition was published in 2012.

3. We reviewed the criteria for drawing — "Big, bright, and bold." On the word wall there were now cards each with the name of a child. One by one the children selected their name card on their own or with help from a teacher. They showed or read their name to their A-B partner.

4. We modeled what we liked to do with our families by acting out the activity. In groups of three or four, the students acted out, for the class, what they liked to do. Those who were not acting watched and tried to guess the activities. All students had a chance to act out their activity. Needless to say, this was a boisterous time with lots of language building.

5. The children then drew something that they liked to do with their family, and we followed a similar conferencing procedure. During the conferences it was apparent that some of the students were working on drawings that reflected the topic of the day while others were drawing something that reflected their interests. Student choice is an important part of Writers Workshop and we believe that each author has a story to tell. We honored and discussed each drawing regardless of whether the student had chosen the class topic. The criteria for drawing and writing remained the same, something reinforced through the feedback shared with the child.

Day 3: Exploring Things We Can Do

1. We discussed things that children did on their own at home and things that they needed help to do. A class list of *things that we can do on our own* was compiled on chart paper and each child was encouraged to add something that he or she could do. One of us recorded a word or phrase that each child used while the other teacher quickly drew a picture showing that activity next to the word or phrase.

2. We chorally "read" the list using the visual pictures and the words or phrases.

3. We modeled an A-B discussion about something that each of us needed help to do when we were growing up and who helped us. The children then moved into A-B partners to share an example of something they needed help with at home and identify who helped them.

4. We then compiled a list of *things that we need help to do* using words, phrases, and drawings. We read the list together.

5. In their Writers Workshop notebooks, the children drew and wrote about things that they could do on their own or things that they needed help to do. In addition to using the criteria for drawing, the children were invited to add letters or sounds (many of which they borrowed from their names). When we met with each child during a conference, we supported each child in writing a few letters or numbers from memory or from around the classroom.

Day 4: Drawing a Story of Play

1. We showed several books with a variety of illustrations or photos of children playing with other children or adults and discussed the illustrations. We modeled, then encouraged the children to make personal connections to the illustrations with their A-B partners.

2. We wrote *I play* on the board, and one by one the children added a word or phrase about what they liked to play or with whom they liked to play. Again, we recorded the words or phrases and made quick drawings.

3. As we recorded simple words such as *tag* and *ball*, we verbally stretched out the word so that the sounds within the word were more easily heard. The class repeated the stretched-out word and children who were starting to record letter sounds wrote some of the sounds they heard on the board. We were not concerned with correct spelling. The focus was on connecting sounds with letters; the goal was to nudge children to notice that words help to express ideas and that sounds can be represented by letters.

4. We read the list of *I play* responses together, then the children drew a story about themselves playing with a family member or friend. They were reminded to make their drawings "big, bright, and bold" and to print their names next to the drawings of themselves. This was a noisy writing time with children sharing their stories as they worked in their notebooks.

5. The *I play* list of words generated during this lesson was added to the word wall, with *I Play* as a subtitle.

6. As the children worked, we circulated, conferencing with each, recognizing their thinking and their work, extending their oral language, and writing and reading their question.

Day 5: Noticing Detail

1. We chose examples of student drawings that met any of the class criteria for being big, bright, or bold and some student work that included letters, strings of letters, or words. In groups of three, children examined one of the examples. The question that each group discussed as members looked at the example was, "What do you notice?"

2. Each group showed their example and told the class what they noticed about the artwork or writing.

3. As the children shared this information, we recorded their words and phrases to provide more detail about how to draw or write effectively. Their descriptions helped us gauge how much they understood of the class criteria and helped our English language learners be immersed in the formal language.

4. The examples were displayed around the classroom, and the children did a Gallery Walk, seeing and talking about each example.

5. Back in A-B partners, the children told each other what they had noticed in the examples and what they now wanted to add to their own drawing or writing.

6. Before leaving the carpet, the children each shared what they were going to draw and write about. They were given this reminder: "Tell a story using big, bright, bold drawings and include words and letter sounds."

7. As we conferenced, we asked what the child had added to his or her writing or drawing based on the student examples and what the child wanted us to notice. Doing this allowed us to reinforce both criteria for success and author ownership and control.

We want all our learners to see themselves as able and capable, to recognize what they are doing well, and to set plans for more learning.

Future Days: Sharing Stories of Our Lives

Throughout the term we collaborated to assess the strengths and needs of individual students by comparing the child's work to a writing performance standard designed for early primary students. We also discussed class-wide trends, both in terms of learning strengths and areas for growth. We used this information to co-plan future Writers Workshop lessons.

Beyond that, we encouraged children, as they were able and interested, to add letters, numbers, or words, to use words from the word wall, or to add sounds to label their drawing. In our diverse class, a few of our students were already experimenting with print. Many were not and some were not used to even holding a pencil. In the first term of the school year, few of our children were independently adding print to their drawings.

By the second term of the year, in addition to calling for drawings that were "big, bright, and bold," we broadened the criteria to include the addition of words and letters to represent the sounds they heard in words. By bringing students' attention to letter–sound associations and word identification, we helped their emergent writing and reading skills expand in a natural way.

Since this first class, we have taught children who have lived in refugee camps and children who have experienced trauma in leaving their families and country of origin. Doing so has reminded us of the importance of being sensitive to our students and our topic selection. We have also used this sequence with topics such as what we like to eat and what we like to play.

We have been very pleased with the results from this intensive collaboration at the beginning of the year. Working together has helped us better create community, better learn about and respond to our students, and better create a vibrant environment for writing and sharing and talking. All the children in our class saw themselves as successful writers. They gained confidence and competence in their oral and written communication. We learned so much about one another as we shared stories of our lives.

A Team Collaboration: Grades 6 and 7

During the first term of a school year, co-author Leyton Schnellert, as learning resource teacher, collaborated with four Grades 6/7 classroom teachers who shared his beliefs about students needing to feel that they belong in the classroom. Their goal was to engage middle-years students in improving their writing while becoming "self" and "other" wise.

The initial questions of the Grades 6/7 teachers had propelled them into an inquiry project that shaped their instruction for the term.

> *Chris Loat*: "How can I streamline my writing program to help all of my students feel more successful? I have many strategies for writing but I don't think all of my students are reaching their potential."
>
> *Rick Hikida*: "How can I help my students generalize the skills and knowledge they learn from one piece to the next? I have tried to introduce the Performance Standards to the students, but it doesn't seem to make a difference."
>
> *Andrea Western/Cesca Juhasz* (job-share partners): "How can we achieve a balance between choice and demand topics? Our students write well when given a topic, but struggle with significantly less powerful writing when choosing a topic of their own."

We were already committed to the writing process. Planning and teaching together, however, gave us an opportunity to refine our skills and better address the needs of our diverse groups of students.

A Focus on Belonging

We met on the last day of school in June and sketched out our plan for the following fall. We knew that our incoming groups of students had trouble getting along, so we decided that weaving in aspects of social responsibility and perspective taking would be crucial for a successful school year. The school had already begun developing an effective positive behavior approach, and so we planned to embody the acronym STAR (Safety, Teamwork, Accountability, Respect), adopted by the school, in our lessons and interactions with the students. We decided to begin the fall with personal, or impromptu, writing that would allow us to get to know the students — each individual's point of view and interests — while focusing on meaning and ideas in their writing. We chose the topic of belonging for the first term.

As a starting point, we reread chapter 3 on belonging from Faye Brownlie and Judith King's *Learning in Safe Schools*, second edition, and adapted some of the activities for our classes.

Our available resource time was minimal — one 80-minute block per class per week. This time was used for co-teaching. Often, the learning resource teacher would model an anchor lesson in one of the classes. Following the anchor lesson, the classroom teachers shared what had happened, then worked with the same strategy and learning intention at least twice more before the next anchor lesson a week later. Each anchor lesson included

- time for a mini-lesson
- time for students to begin writing
- time for students to share excerpts from their work in progress

The writing blocks between anchor lessons were usually 40 minutes each, with a quick review of the anchor lesson and time to write and share.

Week 1: Pre-writing

Anchor Lesson: Getting to Feelings and Emotions through Pre-writing

The brainstorm allowed us to show the students several things:
- that a brainstorm is one way to organize thinking
- that one can belong in different ways
- that, in brainstorming, one can add details and explanations to original ideas

1. As learning resource teacher, I modeled an individual brainstorm on "what belonging means to me," giving examples from my life of places, activities, and people that have made me feel as if I belonged. I sought to cover a variety of areas that students could relate to — sports, music, religion, family, school, and leisure activities. Modeling the inclusion of the fullest range of places and people helped students tap into the same things.

2. Students generated their own brainstorm on belonging.

3. I used a different color to write how each of my points made me feel; students then did the same on their brainstorms.

In this web, the student has identified family, church, clubs, and his house as centres of belonging and explained, for example, "I know I belong here because my family is here and I was living here for a long time."

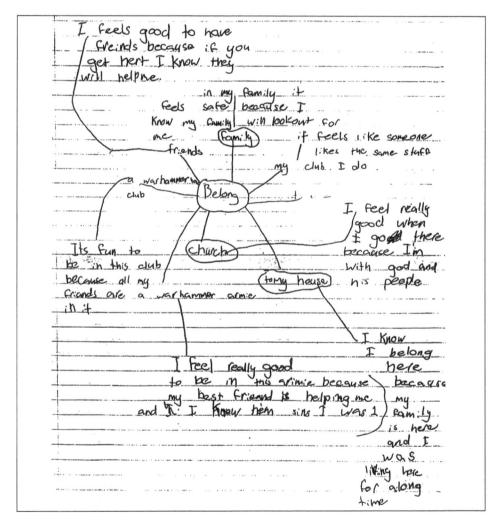

4. I circled the three ideas that I thought were my best, most powerful ideas, and prompted the students to circle their three best ideas. The classroom teacher then asked me to elaborate further on my ideas, and in a third color I wrote down more information that came from this discussion.

5. Students took out a third color. They shared and discussed their top three examples with the others in their table group of four. With the new color, students added to their brainstormed lists ideas that came up in the group.

6. Students were given the journal topic "What does belonging mean to me?" I modeled writing on the Smart Board and asked the students to write their own pieces.

7. I quickly finished my piece and then, with the other teacher, circulated around the room to nudge students who needed assistance in getting started, often referring to the example on the Smart Board.

We learned a great deal from observing students' writing. For example, after the first week my partners Cesca and Andrea noted the following:

Class writing strengths:

- they enjoy writing
- excited to talk about social issues and real-life situations
- have a lot of ideas/things to write about
- no one was sitting staring at their paper saying, "I have nothing to write about . . ."

Areas to work on:

- they use very simple vocabulary (e.g., *nice, mean, sad*)
- getting more depth/feeling in their writing (many would express ideas orally but did not convey that same sense in their writing)

Over the course of the next week, students wrote entries on friendship: "What does being a good friend look like? sound like? feel like?"

After the first week, we decided to develop criteria with students to help address their writing needs and our inquiry questions. We would spend the next six to eight weeks gently developing criteria with the students.

Week 2: Establishing Writing Criteria

Anchor Lesson: Analyzing Peer Writing for Strengths

Once students internalize and articulate what makes powerful journal writing, which is a type of personal, or impromptu, writing, they should apply these criteria, writing fluently and confidently without stopping too often to attend to the criteria.

1. With a What Makes a Journal Entry Powerful? graphic organizer in front of them, we looked at three student samples pre-selected by the classroom teacher, analyzing them to determine what makes a powerful journal entry. These samples represented a range of ability levels, each showing something powerful.

2. As we looked at the samples, we asked students to identify qualities that made each journal entry powerful. Students then individually put the aspects that they thought were most important in the "My Ideas" section of the graphic organizer. We asked students to circle or otherwise mark their criteria to rate the top three criteria in order of importance.

3. In table groups of four, students shared their ideas and recorded them in the "Group Ideas" section of the graphic organizer. Groups then came to a consensus on their top three criteria and shared these with the class. These were recorded in the "Class Ideas" section. (See one student's idea summary next page.)

4. After discussing the criteria, students brainstormed and wrote journal entries on this question: "What can belonging look like and feel like in our classroom?"

Class Lessons

Using the criteria that the students had generated, each classroom teacher created follow-up lessons designed to address the needs of their particular class.

Criteria for Powerful Writing: Andrea and Cesca's class

Andrea and Cesca's class looked at more student samples and came up with two or three powerful things about each person's writing sample. Students wrote in their journals after discussing the criteria again. Cesca had three students display the criteria, outlined below, on a poster.

- Put your own feelings into it
- Have details
- Use your imagination
- Use a variety of words
- Interest the reader
- Has a beginning, middle, and an ending
- Own original ideas
- Exciting
- Strong words and ideas
- Consistently written (strong/powerful all the way through)

Focus within a Paragraph: Rick's class

Rick decided to do an anchor lesson to help students stay focused within their paragraphs. He showed a picture of a professional hockey player scoring a goal. He asked students to infer and brainstorm what they knew about the picture and recorded their ideas on the board. Then he modeled writing a paragraph using their ideas while keeping the image of the hockey game on the screen. As a class the students added to his paragraph and read it aloud several times.

Once he completed the paragraph of the hockey game, Rick slid a picture of Long Neck Fred, one of Shel Silverstein's cartoon characters, into the hockey scene. The students had a chuckle over this. Rick asked, "Does Long Neck Fred belong here?" After much discussion, Rick explained that this is what some of the students' paragraphs looked like. There were sentences or ideas that did not belong in the context of the specific paragraph; instead, they should have been included in another paragraph or perhaps made part of a new journal topic. The insertion of Long Neck Fred into the hockey picture was a visual way of showing them what a proper paragraph should look like.

Understanding of Criteria: Chris's class

Chris found that students had some very insightful thoughts and ideas that they were trying to express; however, many seemed unable to express their thoughts in descriptive or meaningful ways. The word *good* seemed to come up far too often. They finished their "Belonging in the Classroom" journal entry and

The student has identified three top personal ideas and three top group ideas about what makes a journal entry powerful.

My Ideas
2 * good detail
* thoughts
* feelings
1 * real events
3 * good examples
* friends & relatives
* good explanations

Group Ideas
* friends & relatives
* friends support you
1 * good explanations
2 * thoughts
3 * feelings
*

Class Ideas
* feelings
* detail
* thoughts
* interesting/description
* good explanations
* real events

Students need to build criteria, then practise writing and revising with the criteria in mind, to become more powerful writers.

worked on another journal response about friendship. Chris and his class discussed the criteria and, during each writing session, he asked students to point out the criteria they felt were important. Chris emphasized that these were the criteria they should think about when writing their responses. After perusing a few of the responses, however, he found that some of the students did not seem to know exactly what some of the criteria — such as use of detail and providing good explanations — referred to.

Chris also noticed that during other written assignments, such as a major Social Studies activity, the students did not seem to realize that they should apply the writing process to their responses: the students immediately began a good copy response without any planning or drafting. Chris stopped the whole class and told them that, for this fairly major assignment, he expected some sort of pre-writing with later revision. Their blank stares of bewilderment at this were telling, as we realized the lack of carry-over in student writing processes from subject to subject.

After two weeks, we were pleased to note that some of the students seemed to be writing in organized paragraphs or sections without a receiving a mini-lesson on the topic. Some had even begun organizing their work into sections with subtitles. By our simply surfacing and emphasizing the criteria, students had begun to move away from writing one long, drawn-out paragraph.

Week 3: Working as a Group

Anchor Lesson: Sorting and Categorizing Criteria

We are smarter together. As we work in teaching teams, we build in student learning teams.

We came up with easy-to-remember names for the criteria:
Final Touch: good sentences, organized, easy to read, neat
Thinking It Through: feelings, pictures/drawings, thoughts, real events
Sounds Great: exciting, good explanations; interesting, descriptive detail; good use of words

1. Each group of four students was given an envelope containing the powerful journal criteria brainstormed the week before. Each idea was typed on its own strip of paper. Students had to deduce which ideas went together and come up with a reason or title for each group. We showed a copy of the strips using a document camera.

2. As a class we analyzed each group's proposal, focusing on which criteria went together, and listed the titles on the Smart Board. We chose the titles that worked best for the class and left them on the overhead. The groups went back and regrouped the criteria using the same process. Each group chose the criteria that they were most certain about and shared their reasoning with the class. Following the students' suggestions, I arranged and rearranged the criteria under the various headings.

3. We asked the students to spend five minutes discussing how effectively they had worked as a group that day.

4. Students then wrote a journal entry responding to this prompt: "How do good groups work?"

Class Lessons

The teachers used the prompts "What makes you a good friend?" and "How can a group make good decisions?" for the week's journal writes. They continued to ask students to choose and focus on two or three criteria for each write, and in one-on-one or small-group conferences gave descriptive feedback as students requested.

Week 4: Using the Criteria

To prepare for this lesson the teachers asked their students to identify a piece of their own writing that they believed met one of the criteria categories particularly well. By this time, students had at least six entries to choose from, and many of them spent more than an hour choosing which piece to use. Those students who struggled with this process sat in partners or small groups while a teacher read their pieces aloud and helped them discuss which criteria they believed had been met. This exercise prepared them for the next anchor lesson when they would continue to use the criteria with their writing.

Anchor Lesson: The Art of Noticing

As learning resource teacher to the three classes, Leyton Schnellert conducted the anchor lesson using one of his own writing drafts.

1. I read one of my draft pieces of writing from the Smart Board. I referred to the posted criteria and read my piece again, looking for an example of one of the criteria.

2. Working in partners, students looked for other examples of the criteria in my piece. We debriefed, and the pairs of students came up to underline a relevant section and label it with the criteria.

3. Students each brought out the piece they had selected. Using a colored pen, they underlined phrases or sentences that they believed demonstrated a criterion and recorded this criterion beside it in the "Teacher Comments" section.

4. Each student shared aloud an excerpt, and the class guessed which criterion it was an example of.

We required each student to have at least one piece a week to work with for the anchor lesson.

5. Students described what they had noticed about their thinking and chose one of the criteria to focus on in their next piece of writing; some students, however, benefited more by returning to finish a piece rather than by starting a new one.

The student has underlined three sections that she believes demonstrate effective use of criteria.

Journal

Title: What does it look & feel like to belong in a group?

Teacher Comments

To belong to a group feels great. Everyone knows your name, welcomes you and hangs out with you. In my group of friends I feel that everyone understands me and cares. When I'm in a class like, for example Judo class, everyone recognizes me and feels challenged and excited to learn new skills together. In my family, I feel loved and cared for. I also look a lot like my dad. When I joined a get-together once, there was no one I knew in the crowd. I was going to leave until I saw my friend and her sister. I stayed and we had lots of fun together. In the school band I feel like I belong because everyone there knows how to play an instrument, and we're all being

feelings

Good / Thoughts Explanations

Real Events / Details

Class Lessons

During the next week the classroom teachers had students look for examples of criteria in their writing and required students to set a goal related to the criteria before each write.

Week 5: Revising

Our definition of revising is to use criteria to help your reader better understand your written message.

We had been focusing on building student confidence, raising awareness of strength in every student's writing, and developing criteria in "kid friendly" language. To prepare for revision, I took the criteria and titles and made a graphic organizer for students (see the filled-in portion on page 87). Now that we had developed their critical eye for linking criteria to examples, we wanted to move students into using these criteria to revise their work. We defined *revising* as using criteria to determine how we, as writers, might better get our messages across.

Anchor Lesson: Making Revisions in Your Writing

1. I explained that, as a writer, I am constantly revising aspects of my writing. I choose a piece or an aspect of my writing that I am excited about and I consider what I know about powerful writing — my criteria — to see if I can make it better.

2. I modeled the process of choosing one really good sentence from my piece. I explained that I was looking for phrases that are or could be descriptive or powerful.

3. I read the first chunk of my piece several times before choosing a sentence to focus on.

   Deep, honest, complex . . . My friend Kara and her husband have a lot on their plate with a baby coming and the restaurant's grand opening on the 22nd.

   I wrote this sentence in the "Good Start" section of my graphic organizer.

4. Students became A-B partners. Partners were asked what they thought could be done to make my sentence more descriptive. I thought aloud and shared my ideas of what I could do. I then revised my sentence using their advice and wrote it in the "Even Better" section.

5. I directed the students to find a sentence from their writing and share it with their partners, telling what they chose and how they would change it.

6. We repeated this oral rehearsal process. Students then chose this or another sentence to write in the organizer and revise.

7. We finished the class by having students share the first and revised versions of their sentences.

Here is an excerpt from a teacher-made line master that shows how one student went from Good Start to Even Better to Wow!

Good Start	Even Better	WOW!
My last interest is collecting hockey cards, I have about 1000 hockey cards which include my favourites. My favourites are Wayne Gretzky, Mark Messier and Curtis Joseph. When I am collecting I look and feel excited when I find a sweet card.	My last interest is collecting hockey cards. I have about 1000 hockey cards which include some of my favourites. Three of my favourites are Wayne Gretzky, Mark Messier and Curtis Joseph. When I am collecting I look and feel excited when I find a good card. The best card I've ever found was a Bobby Orr rookie card. When I found the card I was so excited I wouldn't stop talking about it.	My last interest is collecting hockey cards. I have over 1000 hockey cards which include some of my favourites. Three of my favourites are a Wayne Gretzky, a Mark Messier and a Curtis Joseph rookie card. When I'm collecting hockey cards I look and feel excited when I find a great card like my Curtis Joseph. So far the best card I've ever got was a Bobby Orr rookie card. I was so satisfied I couldn't stop talking about it. And to date I still tell my friends about it.

Class Lessons

Students continued to write and revise aspects of their pieces over the next week. They were required to conference with teachers before they could revise their sentence(s) a second time and take them to the Wow! stage. Students then conferenced on each other's work to describe what kinds of revisions had been done. Finally, they each went back to the section of the piece that their sentence was from and revised the section in reference to a category of the criteria. They handed in the revisions to the classroom teacher. These pieces let us know what we needed to focus on next with our mini-lessons; they allowed us to give students specific feedback on how they were doing according to our specific goals, and how they could get better.

Up to and including this time, no marks had been given. We were in assessment for learning mode. Students did not submit pieces for evaluation (assessment of learning) until the end of the term.

Week 6: Choosing Topics

We wanted to stimulate more discussion regarding content, and to reinforce that writers need passion for their topic and voice in their writing. We also wanted to offer more student choice of writing prompts.

Prompts included these:
- Imagine what a school would be like if all children felt they belonged.
- Tell about a time when you were being judged.
- Tell about a time you didn't belong.
- Describe what cooperation means.
- Think about how this school includes everyone.
- Imagine what being new in this class would be like.

Anchor Lesson: Graffiti and Conversation

1. We reviewed the criteria as a class. We gave students a choice of two criteria categories to target: meaning and style.

2. The class was divided into six groups. Each group was given a "graffiti palette" (a large piece of butcher paper) with a different "Belonging" prompt

in the centre. Students had between 5 and 10 minutes to brainstorm their reactions, examples, and details to the prompt on the graffiti palette before rotating to the next topic. Students returned to their original palette after three rotations.

3. Students examined the results, taking turns reading quotes from the graffiti.

4. Each student then chose one of the prompts to write about independently. Students were provided with a Journal Organizer, with a thinking space for drawing, listing, and mind mapping.

Here, a student has sketched and drafted a paragraph about refereeing based on the prompt "Tell about a time when you were judged."

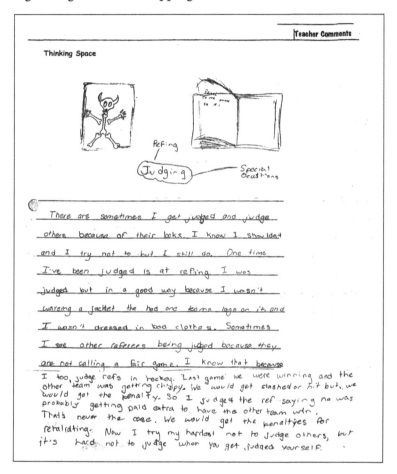

Class Lessons

Our Grades 6/7 team brainstormed related themes for the rest of the term and chose "Peace/Piece" as a relevant Social Studies and Science infused twin focus. By this time, students were familiar with the routines of journaling and felt an ownership of the criteria. We asked each class to brainstorm a list of powerful journal topics related to the concept of peace. First, though, we read a powerful picture book about the 9/11 attacks in the United States. On page 89 is the impressive, but abridged list from one of the classes. Notice how almost all of the ideas are not only powerful but are posed as prompts.

The picture book was *I Survived the Attacks of September 11, 2001*, written by Lauren Tarshis and illustrated by Scott Dawson.

Peace Journal Topics

I get angry when . . .

I feel peaceful when . . .

If Hitler never existed, how would the world be different?

If peace was a law, would you obey it?

Will the world ever have total peace?

Do you think that wars between countries end in peace?

Do you think the world will be without wars?

Will terrorism ever end?

Can war ever result in peace?

Do you think that everyone in schools wearing uniforms would stop bullying?

Do you think that you have a reason to revolutionize the world in peace?

If you were able to change anything in the world, what would it be?

If money did not exist, would the world have peace?

Make peace, not war.

Make friends, not war.

What is peace?

What is war?

What is love?

What are friends?

What is a perfect world?

What is freedom?

Do people think better of themselves or of each other?

Do weapons help create peace?

How can we heal the world?

Will war become helpful?

Will terrorists rule the world?

War will not settle anything.

Do you care more about war than peace?

Do you think children's lives will be affected by war?

If you could make world peace, would you?

Do you think terrorists care?

I used to think that peace was . . . but now I know that peace is . . .

What do you think the world would be like without peace?

Do you think countries resolve their differences in war and fighting? Why or why not?

What positive things have been achieved since Sept. 11, 2001?

What do you think "peace" means? Why?

Do you think that fighting with each other helps us realize why peace is important?

Be helpful, don't be greedy.

Will racism lead to peace?

How do you feel about Sept. 11th?

How do you feel about enemies?

How do you feel about bombing Afghanistan?

How do you feel about friendship?

Do you want to help the world?

Do you want to help starving people? people in need? the homeless? sick people? orphans?

Why is the world like this?

Why are there evil people?

Why is there war?

Do you care about people with disabilities?

What do you want to do about the world?

What do you want to do about wars?

If I could change something, it would be . . . (how people think about each other, sin, etc.)

What is your vision of peace?

What would a non-racist world look like?

If terrorist attacks had never happened, do you think there would be more peace in the world?

If there were less killing, would there be more peace in the world?

Do you think peace should be a right? Why or why not?

What do you think is achieved from war?

Pray for peace, not war.

Do you think spending millions making weapons is going to make peace?

Week 7: Using Form Effectively

After reading through the first peace journals we decided that a very targeted mini-lesson was in order. Students were doing a good job including details and emotions, but the pieces read almost like lists. Students were not fully expanding their ideas. We also noticed that most pieces did not have a satisfying ending. We realized that we had supported the students in writing multi-paragraph pieces, but needed to have a targeted lesson on effective ways to use form, which encompasses organization, sequence of ideas, beginning, middle, and end.

Anchor Lesson: Moving beyond Listing to a Full Focus

1. We chose two magazine articles that had effective leads and endings and told the story of one key moment. We read these and discussed their form and if and how the authors gave reasons and explanations for their details and examples.

2. We looked at the list of peace topics generated. In partners, students discussed how to choose a topic that would yield the best personal writing.

3. I modeled an initial web about my chosen topic, getting down several possible ideas. The students chose a topic from the peace prompt list and did the same.

4. I returned to my web and thought aloud about which of my ideas I had really strong examples for. I wrote down the powerful example, explaining the connection between the prompt and my idea. I explained that one strong personal example is the basis for the entire piece. I generated several possible leads and started my piece on the Smart Board.

5. Students then wrote their entries.

Students easily chose a topic and began to brainstorm ideas. We were impressed with the quality of questions and the variety of ideas around the theme of peace. When it came time to write, they all got ideas down on paper. Some of them were really focusing on powerful, catchy beginnings, detailed middles, and endings that tied up their writing.

Class Lessons

The mini-lesson really seemed to sink in for many of the students. However, given some of the topics, it was difficult for them to focus only on one example, rather than to give a list. Some of the students lacked enough background knowledge or information to write in detail about one example. This became something to focus on for the next week: choosing a topic that students had a strong opinion about or examples to use in their writing.

The teachers re-emphasized that we wanted to stretch out a moment and work on adding details and explanation in our personal writing. They also modeled effective endings and had students examine and rework their leads and endings. The classes decided that effective endings included opinions, questions, and observations.

Whenever Writers Workshop time was scheduled, the students had a focus. They were getting better at choosing a topic and were coming up with personal stories or illustrative examples. Teachers and students concluded that writing more than one extended example helped create a powerful, longer entry.

Using a key moment to build on with description and detail will yield a much stronger piece than a list.

Week 8: Establishing Criteria for Evaluation

About five weeks into the process, we had explained to students that they would be selecting three pieces to take to an almost published form. Evaluation of these, combined with that of a "demand write," would constitute their writing mark for the term. We reviewed the rubric with the class. Students were then given a copy of the rubric to refer to while finalizing their writing.

As we moved towards the end of the term, we could see how our identifying patterns in our students' writing led to focused mini-lessons which, in turn, resulted in immediate improvement in the students' writing. Targeted teaching was making a difference!

Anchor Lesson: Getting Ready for Evaluation

1. Each teacher and class revisited the criteria and the original categories and refined them. They then looked at the two sets of criteria — the class's revised criteria and the provincial performance standards — to see where there was overlap.

2. Each class combined the criteria into one master set (that for Chris's class appears below). We asked the students what they thought we should add to the criteria based on our recent mini-lessons. In the end we had a category and descriptors that matched each of the four aspects of writing on the performance standards, each built by looking at pieces by us and other authors.

3. To parallel the performance standards, we added a fourth column to our Good Start, Even Better, Wow! rubric, and called it "I'm There." We clarified what a strong piece would include and put these descriptors in the "I'm There" column. We did not generate descriptors for the other columns. We focused on "I'm There" (what would be considered "Fully Meeting" on our provincial Performance Standards for Writing).

We believe that the power of generating criteria over time is one of the key reasons that students steadily improved. They had determined the descriptors, constantly worked towards the criteria, and now had refined them. The students had absolute ownership over their own set of criteria.

Writing that earns a Wow! typically involves critical and creative thinking and has rich vocabulary. The writing stands out as unique.

Our Journal Criteria

	Good Start	Even Better	I'm There	Wow!
Thinking It Through feelings, thoughts & opinions real events explanations & details personal experiences			• fully explains why you have these opinions, thoughts or feelings • feelings and thoughts fully support the topic • reader clearly understands the thoughts/opinions of the writer • deeper level of thinking that shows insight and individuality	
Sounds Great description good use of words clear explanations varied length of sentences			• uses clear and varied vocabulary • variety of sentence length and structure • language helps the reader understand the ideas and thoughts of the writer	
Get Up & Organized well organized ideas interesting beginning well developed middle powerful ending one main idea in each paragraph			• ideas flow from one to another in a logical sequence • interesting beginning • well developed middle • powerful ending • related ideas are grouped together	
Final Touch sentences - mechanically correct COPS			• most sentences are grammatically correct • few errors in capitalization, punctuation and spelling • errors do not interfere with the meaning of the journal	

Mr Loat's grade 6/7 class

4. Once the categories and descriptors were revised, the students looked at some of their own work to find samples that fit the specific criteria.

What We Evaluated

For evaluation, most students chose pieces that they had already revised parts of during our various mini-lessons. Eventually, we evaluated the following for each student:

1. three journal entries that they worked through the three stages — taking their writing from a "Good Start" to "Even Better" to "I'm There"

2. an in-class write (If students needed additional time to finish, we blocked off extra time in class.)

Thinking Back, Looking Ahead

We were thrilled by the progress of our three classes of students. While developing an understanding of what is important in personal, or impromptu, writing, they also learned how to analyze their writing with specific criteria in mind. The students demonstrated a good understanding of the rubric that we came up with collaboratively.

Journal writing continued throughout the year; however, in term 2 we shifted our focus to story writing. We found the process of generating criteria and building a rubric to take far less time. Students were amazed to find that many of the criteria were the same and that all of the criteria categories were similar. As we moved through the term, targeting and modeling specific aspects of writing in our mini-lessons, we found that students revised their writing more successfully. This was especially true for some of our struggling writers. Our explicitness about what worked in writing, building from what was needed in their writing, was most beneficial to them.

One of our initial questions, the one raised by Rick — "How can I help my students generalize the skills and knowledge they learn from one piece to the next?" — seemed to answer itself, as students began to point out the importance of the skills and the transferability of the criteria from piece to piece and genre to genre. We had learned how to work together as a community of writers. In addition to partners, our classes could now work in trios and quartets. Through our topic of belonging we were able to bring to the surface what each of us believed belonging to be and how this concept applied in the classroom, in the community, and in our personal lives. We, as teachers, discovered that we were more comfortable slowing down and focusing on developing key skills. Finally, we all had begun to ask one another for the reasons behind our examples, our actions, and our statements. We were all learning to look for our expanded stories, instead of just creating lists.

6 The Class Novel

The traditional practice of choosing one novel for all students is based on the belief that, if everyone is doing the same thing, all are included.

In our intermediate, middle-years, and senior-years classes, the class novel has too often become the backbone of the English Language Arts program. Teaching a novel usually means analysis and close examination of literary elements, such as the plot line, the author's intent, and literary techniques. A whole-class novel is manageable. The same assignments are used for everyone. Everyone is working at the same time, in the same place, at the same pace. It is traditional. It takes up time.

Reconceptualizing the Class Novel

Novel study can be a worthwhile activity is it is
- brief
- well introduced
- adapted to class needs
- encouraging and supportive of students' independent reading
- encouraging of conversation among students

We believe that the time has passed when one size fits all. One of the challenges of today's diverse classes is that, when a teacher chooses one novel for the entire class, rarely can all the students actually read the novel. So the teacher, in an attempt to include everyone in discussions about the novel, reads it to them, chapter by chapter. Two things then happen:

- Much time is devoured.
- Most students engage in almost no reading.

These results neither promote personal growth in reading nor create conditions for developing an enthusiasm for and a love of reading. The able readers are bored; the less able readers are dormant.

Beliefs to Govern Novel Teaching

We *do* believe that teaching a novel to the entire class can be a worthwhile activity; however, we have come to rely on a set of beliefs for this teaching:

- The novel study should take three to four weeks at a maximum; otherwise, students will not have enough time to read.
- The novel needs to be introduced in a way that sets up all students to want to read it and be better able to read it.
- Not every chapter needs to be processed in the same depth, that is, assigned a strategy, discussed, and worked over.
- Not every literary technique or comprehension strategy needs to be covered in every novel. Teachers are wise to choose a theme, a technique, or a focus, and address this in one novel, knowing that they can address other curriculum goals using other texts.
- Students need to read independently as much as they can.

- Comprehension questions, chapter by chapter, take up valuable time and teach nothing.
- The purpose of a novel study is to become engrossed in a good read, not to do "stuff" such as comprehension questions and book reports.
- A whole-class novel is an appropriate time to introduce, teach, model, and practise a reading/thinking strategy that students can later use in their independent reading.

Connecting: Building Background Knowledge

Several strategies build background knowledge and increase a student's interest and motivation to read. Teachers may choose to use one or more of these strategies, depending on the needs of their students. The strategies are usually the students' first introduction to the novel and precede naming the text or any preamble about it.

Gallery Walk

1. Collect a series of images or artifacts that represent the setting of the novel, or things that are particularly important to the characters in the novel. Place them around the room, arranged so that students in groups of three can meet to examine them. For a class of 30 students, therefore, you would display 10 items.

2. In groups of three, students discuss what they are seeing and what it might tell them about the upcoming novel. Students spend about three minutes on each item. They do not need to see all the artifacts — visiting four is plenty.

3. Upon returning to their seats, students write for 10 minutes, explaining what they think they now know about the novel.

4. Student writing is shared with the whole class with all the images or artifacts displayed, so students can predict which images or artifacts each student author examined.

Historical Picture Book

1. Choose a picture book that builds background knowledge about a novel whose setting is not well known to the students in the class. This book can be either historical (when) or geographic (where).

2. As you read the picture book, show the pictures and discuss the language and the images with the students.

3. Read the picture book again, while the students focus on the aspects of facts and connections and make two-column notes:

Historical [or Geographic] Fact	My Connections

Artifacts: From Woven Baskets to Rap

Artifacts to use for a Gallery Walk pertaining to Shirley Sterling's *My Name Is Seepeetza* might include
- a First Nations carving, a mask, a woven basket
- a First Nations beaded suede vest, a piece of silver-carved jewellery, a cedar head band
- quotations from residential school survivors and their families
- a provincial map of the First Nations of British Columbia
- a copy of the 11 June 2008 "Statement of Apology to Former Students of Indian Residential Schools," issued by the government of Prime Minister Stephen Harper
- a listening station of music by War Party from the Cree Nation in Alberta (The music addresses social and political issues through rap lyrics.)

Secret of the Dance by Andrea Spalding and Alfred Scow (illustrated by Darlene Gait) and *Shi-shi-etko* by Nicola I. Campbell (illustrated by Kim LaFave) are both excellent picture books to build background knowledge with a class novel such as *Red Wolf* by Jennifer Dance.

4. Students can work in pairs to embellish their notes, highlighting and noting three to five aspects of either history (when) or geography (where).

5. Hear at least one response from each pair, building a class web focusing on either the *when* or the *where* information.

Choice Beginnings

1. Choose 15 to 20 image-producing words from the novel. Tell students that you are going to read a series of image-producing words from the upcoming novel. Invite them to respond to these words by asking questions, making predictions, or sketching.

2. Invite students to predict which response format they are most likely to use and to tell this to a partner.

3. Read the words to the students several times, inviting them to listen and respond as they are ready. Plan on reading the words as often as five or six times, encouraging the students to listen and respond to them, *not* copy them down.

4. Check to see how many students expected to respond in one way, then responded in another. Hear some of the questions and predictions, and see some of the images.

Processing: Building Meaning

The strategies that follow bear repeating, so students gain skill in using the thinking behind the strategies in their independent reading. However, it is inappropriate to work with a strategy in every novel chapter. That would mean too much teaching and too little time supporting students in working towards independence as thoughtful readers.

Once some background and motivation have been built, some classes are able to begin independently reading the novel. Other classes, however, demand more teacher support with the language, structure, style, or background knowledge needed to fully understand the novel. If this is the case, the first chapter might be read aloud by the teacher, while the students engage in one of the strategies outlined here. These strategies can also be relevant later in the novel, with the teacher reading aloud a chapter or a segment of a chapter that requires additional teaching and the students using the strategy more independently.

Quadrants of a Thought

For Quadrants of a Thought as part of a strategic sequence, see page 21 in Chapter 1.

Filling in two quadrants is enough to begin with, and will grow with practice to include all four quadrants.

1. Students fold a piece of paper in four and label the quadrants Image, Language, Physical Senses, and Emotions.

2. Invite students to record, in two of the four boxes, what is going on in their minds about the text as you read aloud. Students may sketch in the Image quadrant; record significant words, phrases, or quotations in the Language quadrant; record sounds, smells, the sense of touch or movement, and tastes in the Physical Senses quadrant; and note either their emotional reactions or those of the characters in the Emotions quadrant.

3. Read one or two pages of the text, then stop and hear what students have been recording.

4. Make a quadrant on the Smart Board and record the student responses. Tell students that they are not required to copy down what is there, but may use any of the ideas, as they wish.

Recording the class responses develops a whole-class appreciation of what others are thinking and fosters a greater understanding of personal connections and interpretations.

5. Continue the process, stopping again, adding to the class recording. Ask the students to notice what is changing in their thinking and their recording as you continue.

6. Stop and debrief a third time, if appropriate, then read without interruption to the end; or tell the students to finish the chapter reading independently.

Listen, Sketch, Draft

1. Students fold a page into four or six boxes. They will use two boxes for each chunk of text, so you will have to decide how many chunks you will be processing.

2. Read the first part of the chapter after inviting students to sketch what is happening as you read.

3. Stop reading, give a few moments for the sketching to finish, then invite students to share their sketches and their thinking with a partner.

4. Hear samples of the partners' conversations by asking, "What surprised you about your partner's thinking?" or "What did your partner do differently from you?" or "What do you know now that you didn't before your conversation?"

5. Students quickly record, in writing, what is important to remember in the first chunk of text.

6. Continue this process for one or two more chunks, then have students complete the reading of the first chapter independently.

Clustering from Text

1. Read the first few pages of the text to the students. As you read, invite students to quickly cluster their thinking about the text, important words from the text, and their connections to the text.

Students looking for more ideas may ask you to reread the text.

2. Ask students to circle two powerful words in their cluster.

3. Use these powerful words to make a class cluster on the Smart Board. Invite each student to get ready to contribute.

Students are encouraged to contribute an idea, to categorize or connect this idea to others, and to explain why they placed the idea where they did. We call this "because" thinking.

4. As students contribute their ideas, remind them that you can record, but you cannot read their minds, so they need to tell you where to place each idea. In other words, students are categorizing as they build the class cluster.

5. When all have contributed and the board is full, take out colored Smart Board pens. Each student now has a chance to rearrange the cluster by connecting words that were not previously connected and explaining their relationship. This part of the strategy really deepens understanding.

6. Once the cluster is "messed up" and most of the words have been reconnected, students write for 10 minutes in response to what has been read. Expect the writing to demonstrate a thoughtful, connected, powerful understanding.

Processing: Reading with Understanding

We want students to engage in actual reading, to take active part in conversations about the text, to become wrapped up in the novel rather than to experience reading as moving slowly through a text, doing "stuff" about it. Three strategies that can aid students during reading and that work well in sequence are reading with a partner, reading with sticky notes, and writing in response journals.

Partner Reading

If students still cannot independently read the text, we place the students in reading partners for the duration of a class novel study. When assigning a chapter or two to read, the partners work together during class time. The rule is that they need to arrange a way of reading that ensures that each partner reads at least some of every second page — even if it is only a line! We set up the partnerships, considering social issues (who can work with whom) and reading skill (one person able to read longer passages). As the students are reading, we move among the partners, listening in, extending and supporting understanding. This is an ideal time to listen to students read orally and to have mini-conferences with the pairs of students.

Class Conversations Based on Sticky Notes

Sometimes the students just mark the spot with a sticky note; more often they write or draw on their notes.

We encourage students to read with sticky notes in hand, distributing them to the partner groups. Their task, as they read, is to use the sticky notes to mark places in the text where

- there is exquisite language
- a strong emotion is evoked
- a clear image is created
- they are confused and need to ask a question
- they say, "Oh, wow!"
- they find a phrase they want to use

Students take the sticky note from its spot in the novel and place it on their desk as they speak. Then, at a glance, we all can tell who has not yet had a chance to speak and who has.

This tiny strategy causes much literate conversation to occur. When the partners are finished reading, we hold a class conversation based on what is written and drawn on the sticky notes. Many more students participate in this whole-class conversation because they have already rehearsed with their partners. The conversation is less likely to be controlled by a verbal few. We begin our conversations each time with a different focus, sometimes with the "Oh, wow!" statements, sometimes with the images, sometimes with the questions. The focus affects who will speak first in the conversation.

Response Journals

After the class conversation, we move to writing in response journals. All students are better able to participate in writing a thoughtful response because they have been supported before the writing, rather than getting feedback after the writing.

We do not ask comprehension questions as we are progressing through the novel. These are not supportive of developing more thoughtful readers or of increasing reading skill. They are the stuff that kills reading by over-monitoring. They are not real questions, as we teachers already know the answers. We try to engage students in real responses — in explaining their thinking and reactions, and generating their own questions to develop understanding about the novel. (Samples of the kinds of response journals we use are explained in Chapter 7.)

Transforming and Personalizing: Demonstrating Understanding

Thanks to teacher Tina Pali for contributing the *Tuck Everlasting* assignment from her Grades 6/7 class.

The final assignment is assigned by the middle of the novel study, so students can collect information and work with the end in mind. We try to have these assignments open-ended enough that all can participate and can stretch themselves in making new connections.

On the following pages, you will find an assignment for the novel *Tuck Everlasting* by Natalie Babbitt, called "What? So What?" (page 99), and an assignment for *Touching Spirit Bear* by Ben Mikaelsen, which focuses on drama (page 100). Both assignments are appropriate for students in Grades 5 to 10.

What? So What? is a strategy that is accessible to all students and helps them move beyond surface-level thinking — retelling, answering the five newspaper questions — to thinking more deeply about what happens, how characters respond, and why the setting counts. Students have huge choice in deciding on their "what" so the responses are personal and powerful.

WHAT? SO WHAT?
Main Assignment for *Tuck Everlasting*

WHAT?
- Carefully choose a combination of five objects, places, and people that are important to the story.
- Draw, color, and label every object, place, and person.
- For every object, place, and person, write a related quotation from the book and include the page number.

SO WHAT?
- Tell why each object, place, or person is important to the story. Why do you think the author included them in the story? Do they represent something more than meets the eye? An idea? A theme? A value?

CRITERIA
You will earn two marks, one for Art and one for Reading.
Art Mark: The five drawings will go towards your Art mark.
- Your drawings are original, colorful, and detailed.
- They complement your quotation from the book.
Reading Mark (the written work):
- Your quotation from the book matches your drawing.
- Your So What? tells, in your own words, why the object in your illustration is important to the story. This explanation will be about 20–25 words.
- Your explanation goes beyond the obvious.
- Your presentation is neat (published on the computer, or printed or handwritten neatly) and has few errors in conventions.

4 Exceeds Expectations	3 Fully Meets Expectations	2+ Generally Meets Expectations	2 Minimally Meets Expectations	1 Approaching Expectations
• All criteria met • Shows depth, original insights, and connections • Completed with extra care and effort • Outstanding	• Strong, confident work • All criteria met • Very good effort • Completed with care	• Capable work • Most criteria met • More focus needed in depth or clarity • Presentation and/or conventions need more attention	• Some criteria met • Satisfactory work • No extras • Detail and clarity are not yet evident • Presentation and/or conventions need more attention	• Few criteria met

Due Date: Your assignment will be due shortly after completion of the novel. There will, however, be several draft checks prior to the due date, in order to avoid procrastination!

Parent Signature: _____

DRAMA
Main Assignment for *Touching Spirit Bear*

WHAT?
- Work in groups of 2 to 6 students.
- Choose a significant scene from the novel that can be acted out by the number of people in your group.
- Write a script for your scene.
- Practise your script.
- Include props, costumes, and backdrops, as you see fit.
- Be prepared to dramatize your scene for the rest of the class.
- You will have two in-class periods to work on this.

CRITERIA
You will be marked on both your script/scene and on your performance.
Script/Scene Mark:
- The scene chosen is significant within the novel.
- Dialogue matches the author's language or character choice and does not stray from the text.
- All characters have "speaking" parts (or a pseudo voice for the Spirit Bear).
- Script and choice of scene reflect an understanding of the novel.

Performance Mark:
- Voices are audible.
- Characters act while "reading" their lines. (You do not have to memorize your lines, but you should be acting, not just reading the lines.)
- The portrayal of the characters is credible.
- There is appropriate use of props and backdrops.

4 Exceeds Expectations	3 Fully Meets Expectations	2.5 Generally Meets Expectations	2 Minimally Meets Expectations	1 Approaching Expectations
• All criteria met • Shows insight in interpretation • Writing shows individuality of characters • Creates a mood • All group members skillfully involved	• All criteria met • Well interpreted • Writing matches characters • Attempts to create a mood • All group members involved	• Most criteria met • Shows general understanding of the novel • Writing quite plausible • Captures a moment in the novel • Most group members involved	• Some criteria met • Inaccurate interpretation of the novel • Writing needs detail, depth • Mostly retelling • Work appears to have been the result of only a few students	• Few criteria met • Confused understanding of the novel • Undeveloped script or performance • Few students participating

Deeper learning happens when students represent their understanding in different modalities. Drama is a powerful way to process and synthesize ideas.

7 Literature Circles: The Basics, the Big Ideas, and Beyond

Readers who struggle in the intermediate, middle, and secondary years frequently struggle with reading comprehension. We have found a surprisingly high percentage of fluent readers in Grades 6 to 9, but also a disturbingly high percentage of readers struggling with comprehension. We believe that this situation can be improved upon, but in order to do so, we need to better focus our collective efforts on creating conditions to enable more students to become competent, engaged readers.

Conditions That Support Comprehension

Richard Allington, then president of the International Reading Association, spoke at the 2004 fall conference of the Lower Mainland Council of the International Reading Association (LOMCIRA) in British Columbia. Quoting Fielding and Pearson (1994), he identified four conditions necessary to support struggling readers:

1. reading volume

2. high-success reading opportunities

3. engaging in literate conversations

4. useful, explicit strategy instruction

More recent research looks at features of high-engagement environments. As determined by Allington and Johnston (2001) and Pressley (2002), features include the following:

- an available supply of appropriately difficult texts: texts chosen after we know our students, their skills, and their interests
- options allowing students some control over the texts to be read and the work to be accomplished as choice is built into the reading and responding
- the collaborative nature of much of the work, as in literature conversations and dialogue journals
- the opportunity to discuss what was read and written through literature circle conversations and working together with a partner
- the meaningfulness of the activities, which is due to there being room for choice and voice

We believe that our version of literature circles addresses the four conditions and is consistent with the features of a high-engagement environment. Literature circles provide a seamless format within which the learning resource teacher can move in and out of the classroom, co-teaching, joining a literature

Much choice is built into the reading and responding.

See also the book *Grand Conversations, Thoughtful Responses* and the webcast *Literacy in the Middle Years*, Part 2, both by Faye Brownlie.

circle conversation, and supporting individual students as her schedule permits. They are also easily managed alone by a classroom teacher with a very diverse group of students.

1. Reading Volume

There are no limits to how much students can read. Students are encouraged to read as much as they can in school, and at least 30 minutes a night outside of school. Should a student finish a book overnight, he does not wait for other members of his group to catch up. Instead, he exchanges his book for another. If a student is struggling with the reading of a book, the classroom teacher or the learning resource teacher can read with him for a few pages to rekindle interest in the book, build momentum in his reading, coach him to make personal connections, and add to his background knowledge. This can be done without calling a great deal of attention to the student or causing embarrassment, as these book conversations are happening, in some form, as a regular practice in the classroom with all students. The goal is for the students to read and read and read.

2. High-Success Reading Opportunities

Generally, a collection of six copies each of six different titles is sufficient for a class of 30.

A collection of books is chosen with the specific students in mind. Within this selection is at least one title that each student in the class *can* read and will *want* to read. The teacher markets the books by telling the students what kinds of readers will like a certain book (for example, those who love action or are interested in the environment), and what kinds of time and thinking are required to read the book. She also reads an excerpt to give students a feel for the book's language and tone. Prior to reading the excerpts, the teacher invites the students to imagine themselves reading the book.

Students are reminded that they will meet in groups to discuss these books, but that once they finish a book, they move on to another book and another group. Therefore, students need to choose a book that works for them, not for their friends. They will not want to be stuck in a book that does not appeal to them once their friends have moved on.

Able readers often choose easier titles, reading them quickly and returning them to the box. The appeal of these books is then enhanced for more vulnerable readers. They can read something that others also have read or are reading, not just a "special" book for those at-risk.

Students have free choice in choosing their books — even if they are less skilled readers. Generally, we give students a day's grace with their books. If, after a day, the student is not making progress in the book, the teacher can recommend a different book; the reason stated is that the book does not seem to be working for the student, not because the book is too hard. If after two days and some support the student is still not making progress with the chosen title, the teacher asks that the initial book be returned to read at a later date. Student readers are always treated with respect.

3. Engaging in Literate Conversations

Too often, less skilled readers are assigned meaningless tasks, such as comprehension questions or fill-in-the-blank worksheets, requiring little or no sophisticated thinking. These students come to view reading as matching their

Remember that students in conversation groups are all reading in different parts of the book, so their background of the book varies widely.

thinking with someone else's, and believe that someone else always has a right answer. We do not believe that this view of reading is appropriate for any student — and it does not encourage reading. For students to want to read, they need to see value in reading, and for this they need to be treated as readers. Real readers engage in real conversations with others about the books they read. All readers, struggling or otherwise, need the opportunity to talk with others to deepen their understanding and enrich their experience with the book.

To this end, students meet in groups — one group at a time — with the teacher present. The group is defined by those students who are currently reading a specific book; thus, the members of the group are of varied reading skill. Group size is best at five or six students; if too few students are currently reading a certain title, invitations can be extended to those who have finished the book to return to the group and join in the conversation. To come to the group, each student chooses a passage to read to the rest of the group. Once the passage has been read, everyone in the group, including the teacher, "says something" about the passage. If the passage has been stimulating, a free-form discussion will occur once everyone has had a chance to "say something." This free-form discussion is the goal, so sometimes in a group meeting of 15 to 20 minutes, only two students will read their passages. If all get to read, that generally signals the passages did not provoke much discussion.

Expectations for the discussion are simple:

- Each student will participate and no one student can dominate.
- The teacher will model good participant behavior and not take over the group.

Readers who have read further or completed the book are to abide by one rule: tease and tantalize, but do not "spill the beans" of the plot. The students take this rule seriously.

The groups change as students finish books and move on. Readers who read less quickly — often less skilled or less interested readers — end up staying with a group for more conversations around the same title. This easy adaptation builds these students' expertise on the particular book and provides them with more time.

The learning resource teacher can take a group while the classroom teacher takes a different one. While the groups are meeting, the other students read and prepare for their conversations.

The Say Something Strategy

"Saying something" about a passage might involve a group member making a connection, asking a question, describing a reaction to the passage read, or trying to connect the passage to current reading matter.

The Say Something strategy is our way of structuring the conversation so that all can participate. It is our replacement for the more traditional assignment of roles. It is not, however, an end in itself, and as students' skill with inclusive and impassioned discourse grows, the strategy is set aside for a free-flowing conversation. The same thinking applies to the teacher(s) attending the conversation. Although we love being in the conversation — and the students often prefer us there and invite us back to hear our connections — once the students can handle this conversation independently in a way that includes everyone and enriches understanding, they meet on their own.

4. Useful, Explicit Strategy Instruction

Strategy instruction occurs with response journals and with comprehension strategies. Modeling, coaching, and practice opportunities are provided.

Response Journals

Students write in their response journals two or three times a week. The purpose of the journal is for students to reflect on their reading and, in so doing, deepen their understanding. We have had the most success with double-entry journals. We use a progression of double-entry formats.

Double-Entry Journals: Prompt students to fold a page in half and title the left side "What Happened" and the right side "My Thinking." The chart below summarizes what they do on each side of the paper.

What Happened	My Thinking
Choose an event and briefly describe it.	Write your thinking about the event.
OR	
Choose a quotation and record it.	Write your thinking about the quotation.

Students begin by writing equal amounts on both sides, but move to writing less on the left side and considerably more on the right.

The teachers model journal writing by writing in front of the students and having them analyze the writing. As students are writing their entries, teachers can circulate, have quick conferences, and provide descriptive feedback. After making several entries, students offer their own journal writing for analysis. From these samples, criteria are developed to guide subsequent journal writing. Teachers read and respond to most of the journals of younger students, but only weekly to select journals of older students. A teacher responds with descriptive feedback based on the co-created criteria; journals are not given a mark. At the end of the literature circles unit, however, students each select three journal entries to be marked.

Dialogue Journals: We also use the double-entry journal as a dialogue journal (see page 107). In this form, a student writes a letter to a classmate who is currently reading the same book and is in much the same place. The following day, the students exchange their journals and write back to their partners. As with other double-entry journals, the teacher models each phase of the writing: first writing to a partner, then responding in writing to the partner's journal on the following day.

Comprehension Strategies

In middle and secondary grades, teachers and students begin to focus on the techniques the author uses to develop character, plot, and setting.

Every second week, a particular comprehension strategy can be taught to all the students. These comprehension strategies often focus on the story elements of setting, character, and plot. Each time a new comprehension strategy is introduced, it is first taught to the whole class, using a novel which they have all read. Based on this teaching, the class establishes the criteria and marking for the strategy assignment. Students then work on their assignment in class, practising the strategy as it has been taught, working with the criteria, and using the literature circle novel they have just completed reading.

Literature Circles within a Term

Nicole Widdess engaged her Grades 5/6 class in a thematic unit on slavery. Members first built background knowledge about slavery by reading picture books such as Faith Ringgold's *Aunt Harriet's Underground Railway in the Sky* and *Following the Drinking Gourd* by Jeanette Winters. With both of these texts, the students practised the strategy Quadrants of a Thought (see Chapters 1 and 6).

Rather than have her students jump right into literature circles, Nicole gently moved from picture books to a whole-class novel. She used the novel *Rachel: A Mighty Big Imagining* to introduce the Say Something strategy (see page 103) and demonstrate how to have a small-group conversation. She then introduced different books to the students for their literature circles, and then went on to a research inquiry.

Using a Class Novel to Introduce Literature Circle Conversations

- Ask the class to describe what they think literature circles are.
- Record and post student ideas on a Looks Like/Sounds Like chart.
- Explain that students will practise powerful conversations using a class novel. Later they will move into literature circles and have some book choice.
- Preview a novel on the chosen theme, in this case, Lynne Kositsky's *Rachel: A Mighty Big Imagining*.
- Distribute books to the class, one for each two students.
- Read chapter 1 together.
- Assign students to read chapters 2 and 3 with their partners.
- While students are reading, the classroom teacher and the learning resource teacher each meet with a group of six students and discuss chapter 1 using the Say Something strategy.
- After 15 to 20 minutes, have students change groups and discuss in the new groups as much of the text as they have read, using the Say Something strategy.

By dividing the text into two- and three-chapter chunks over the next few days, the teacher can meet with each group once or twice. Each time a meeting is called, the Say Something strategy is used to begin the conversation about the book. After all students have had a chance to respond to the first reading, an open discussion can follow. All students are expected to participate and to come prepared to begin the conversation by reading a quotation from the book. Even though not everyone will have a chance to share a quotation, everyone will have a chance to speak.

After each group has met at least once, discuss with the class, "What makes a powerful conversation about a book?" Record, categorize, and display the students' ideas.

Providing Options through a Text Set

Nicole, her LRT partner, and the school librarian worked together to assemble a thematic text set to provide students with book options for literature circles. They found the National Geographic website on the Underground Railway useful: http://nationalgeographic.org/media/underground-railroad-journey-freedom/. They chose one non-fiction text and two picture books to include in their set, for use in the same way as the more typical novels. A student with Down syndrome and four students who were new English language learners were able to have several conversations with the same two picture books as the rest of the students in the class moved through their groups. Progress for two of the ELL students was so rapid that they could work with an easier novel by the end of the term. These students were then able to choose any of the books, including the picture books, as their focus for the comprehension activities.

A Model Text Set

In her thematic unit on slavery, Nicole found success with these books:

- *Letters from a Slave Girl* by Mary E. Lyons (more challenging read)
- *Sarny: A Life Remembered* by Gary Paulsen (more challenging read)
- *Jump Ship to Freedom* by James Lincoln Collier and Christopher Collier
- *Jip: His Story* by Katherine Paterson
- *Get on Board: The Story of the Underground Railroad* by Jim Haskens (non-fiction)
- *The Maybe House* by Lynne Kositsky (sequel to *Rachel*, easy read)
- *Show Way* by Jacqueline Woodson
- *Day of Tears* by Julius Lester
- *The Glory Field* by Walter Dean Myers (more challenging and for more mature readers)
- *Copper Sun* by Sharon M. Draper (for secondary students)

Nicole recommends these picture book choices for students with special needs and students just beginning to learn English:

- *Barefoot* by Pamela Duncan Edwards
- *O Lord, I Wish I Was a Buzzard* by Polly Greenberg
- *The People Could Fly* by Virginia Hamilton
- *Henry's Freedom Box: A True Story from the Underground Railroad* by Ellen Levine
- *Ellen Craft's Escape from Slavery* by Cathy Moore
- *The Patchwork Path: A Quilt Map to Freedom* by Bettye Stroud
- *Juneteenth for Mazie* by Floyd Cooper
- *Unspoken: A Story from the Underground Railroad* by Henry Cole
- *January's Sparrow* by Patricia Polacco

Nicole moved from a class novel to the books in a text set as outlined here:
- Introduce each book.
- Remind students to be prepared to choose two books, as they may not get their first book choice.
- Use a chart to keep track of who is reading what book.
- Allow students time to read.
- Meet with students in literature circle groups, where each group is reading the same book, calling together one group at a time while the other students continue to read. Use the Say Something strategy to begin the conversation.

Teaching Strategies for Response and Comprehension

The following two strategies help deepen student understanding while reading. Nicole's students engaged in each strategy once a week while reading with their literature circle groups. In the first strategy, two students are each reading the same book and respond to each other's writing about it; in the second, students come up with questions based on the books they are reading and discuss them in literature circles.

Dialogue Journals

- Introduce the concept of the double-entry dialogue journal as letters between friends about the book the two students are reading.
- Model your first entry as a letter on the Smart Board.
- Encourage students to notice what you are writing, how you keep your audience in mind as you write, how you predict, question, seek clarification, and comment on your surprises.
- Students choose a partner who is reading the same book and is in approximately the same place in the book.
- Students write their first entry as a letter to their partner.
- The next day, choose one of the students' journal entries. Write a letter on the Smart Board in response to this student's letter.
- Encourage students to notice how you are responding to what the student has said, and how you extend the student's thinking about the book through your response.
- Students exchange journals and respond to their partner's letter.

Sticky Note Questions

- Students come to this lesson with a question in mind that they have from the book they are reading.
- Using a piece of text from the class novel, model on the Smart Board a question you have. Write the question on a sticky note and place it on the specific part of the text that prompted your question.
- Ask two or three students to demonstrate using a sticky note with a question from their books.
- Encourage students to continue this process independently, finding two or three questions each.
- Prompt students to meet in their literature circle groups to discuss their questions.
- Teachers move among the groups, supporting the inquiry.

Extending Literature Circles into Personal Inquiry

Having read several books, Nicole's students began to build a deeper knowledge about issues related to slavery. They used this knowledge to develop meaningful inquiry questions. The following two strategies support students in developing and investigating their questions.

From Quotations to Thick Questions

- Using the class novel, model how to use information from the novel to generate questions for further research.
- Using a two-column chart visible to the students, record a quotation from the novel that you have a question about.

Quotation	Question

In the Thick of Things

When the question is easy to answer and can be resolved in just a sentence or with a short quotation from one of the books, we call this a "thin" question because it takes little space to answer it. Such a question usually requires students to locate a fact.

When a question is more difficult to answer, we call it a "thick" question because there are many possible explanations and it requires readers to take several quotations or pieces of information to build a reasonable answer.

- Examine the question and ask students to work together in their literature circle groups to find possible answers to the question you have posed.
- Over a week, inquiry groups are asked to record at least five "thick" questions using quotations from their literature circle novels.
- At the end of the week, partners or groups choose one question that they want to research further.
- Students may use the other literature circle books or, with support from a teacher, begin to explore other sources to help develop powerful questions and find related information. Many students choose to use the Internet or non-fiction books displayed in the classroom.

Synthesizing Information

The chosen question (from the five thick questions) is the research question. A good research question will generate new questions and help connect information that students have read and are continuing to read.

- Use a chart such as that on page 110 to model how this question will fuel new questions and connect information, using quotations from the class novel.
- Prompt students to individually record their information on copies of the chart.
- Students meet with their partners or in groups (those with a common research question) to exchange ideas and record them on their charts.

This information is used in the final comprehension activity.

Extending Literature Circles into Dramatic Demonstrations

The final comprehension activity should pull together all that the students have been learning. It helps with closure, before moving on to another topic.

As a final comprehension activity for her slavery unit, Nicole chose to have her students create songs and dramatic scenes that demonstrated their understanding of the history of slavery, the impact it has had on people's lives, and key themes that their books explored. They then performed their work. Students typically need three classes for this.

Criteria-Based Songs

For more examples of arts integration, see *It's All about Thinking: Creating Pathways for All Learners in the Middle Years* by Leyton Schnellert, Linda Watson, and Nicole Widdess.

- Discuss with the students what would make a powerful song about the life of a slave. In other words, what are the students' criteria?
- Record student thinking. It will be used in a final reflection to comment on the message and impact of one another's songs.
- Students choose to work individually, in pairs, or in triads.
- Ask students, using their criteria, to create songs depicting what they think life for a slave would have been like. Have some sample spirituals available.
- Remind students to use words that will evoke the feelings of the slaves. Encourage them to look back at their Four Quadrant organizers and literature circle journals.
- Invite students to perform their songs and listen to those of their peers.
- Ask students to reflect in writing on this question: "How did our songs reflect our criteria?"

Scenes on Big Ideas

- With the students, brainstorm scenes to be included in a musical about slaves.
- Record ideas on chart paper.
- Categorize the ideas into big ideas to help create scenes.
- Determine an order for the scenes. Discuss which of the songs they created could be used in the scenes.
- Have students choose which scene they would like to create. Most students will stay with the groups they wrote songs with, but the groups are flexible.
- Create the scenes and the props in art. As students craft and workshop their scenes, their scene selection may alter, with some scenes being collapsed.

Chapter 5 of *It's All about Thinking*, the 2015 title referenced above, explores this process.

The Production

- Rehearse the whole piece without costumes about five times.
- Have one dress rehearsal.
- Perform for an audience.
- Videotape the performance and watch it together.

Reflecting on Literature Circles

Our experience with literature circles is that more students are reading more of the time. Students are recommending books to each other. They are reading several books in the span of time that a typical novel study takes. They are building their conversation and comprehension skills while also exploring their preferences. What is most important, they are self- and co-regulating their learning: they set goals, make plans, and take action; they then reflect on their plans and actions and adjust for their next conversations and journal entries.

Synthesizing Information

Thinking About . . .	Related Information
Our Question	
New Questions	
Connections	

Pembroke Publishers © 2016 *Student Diversity*, 3rd ed., by Faye Brownlie, Catherine Feniak, Leyton Schnellert ISBN 978-1-55138-318-7

8 Poetry: Three Invitations

It is time to change our approach to poetry. In many classrooms, a match-my-thinking approach to poetry tends to be exclusive, not inclusive.

In many intermediate and middle-school classrooms, poetry is scarcely taught, or it is taught in a very traditional style that relies on the teacher's interpretation of a poem. We want to change this approach to the teaching of poetry. We need to become less apprehensive about the genre, to move beyond a one-right-answer approach, and focus on enjoying and connecting with the poem. In so doing, we include more students and may even encourage students to read poems independently.

1. Thoughtful Discussion

Each reader brings a unique blend of experiences and background knowledge to reading. These experiences and knowledge become the lenses for making sense of, or interpreting, a poem. In discussion groups, students share their interpretations, refine their ideas, discover new ways of looking at a poem, and determine which interpretation works best for them. This networking of thinking is both expansive and supportive. It encourages students to read and respond to poetry and to incorporate the precise language of poetry in their oral and written language.

Here is the process we use to involve students in discussions about poetry:

We prefer poems that present a big idea, invoke strong emotion, or address themes of social justice.

- Read aloud a poem such as "Hiroshima Exit" by Joy Kogawa.
- In heterogeneous groups, students ask each other "I wonder why . . ." questions about words, phrases, or images from the poem.
- Give a copy of the poem to each student.
- Read the poem aloud again. As they listen, students draw, highlight words and phrases, or jot down ideas and questions around the poem.
- In each group a student volunteer rereads the poem aloud a third time. As the students listen, they consider what to say about the poem.

Use student comments to initiate a mini-lesson focusing on some of the poetic devices used in the poem, perhaps imagery, repetition, alliteration, and metaphor.

- Assist students who are learning English and students who are less verbal with prompts:

    I liked these words in the poem . . .
    A picture I have in my mind is . . .
    This poem made me think of . . .
    I wonder about . . .

- One by one, the students in the group share their ideas and the rest of the students listen and reflect upon the comments.
- Prompt students to carefully read again, silently or aloud with the group, focusing on the language choice and the poetic devices.

- Still in groups, students discuss how the poet has used words and phrases in particular ways. Each group tries to reach consensus about what the poem is saying.
- Each group chooses a spokesperson who then explains their interpretation of the poem to the class. Each spokesperson listens carefully in order to build upon or concur with the observations made by the other groups.
- Students complete a five-minute write, contrasting their initial feelings and thoughts about the poem with what they have learned through these discussions.

Evaluation

Throughout this process, the teachers circulate among the groups to provide personalized support to all students, including those students who are having difficulty expressing their ideas due to shyness, limited English, or special educational needs. The teachers listen carefully in order to frame their support in terms of descriptive feedback: a comment on what is working and an extending comment to address what is not working and what is next. The class learns to be supportive and wait for all students to explain their ideas. These skills are necessary for all to develop, as there are times when every learner will need the support of a group in order to achieve clear expression.

These notes are kept to help form term report-card comments on communication and working with others.

This is an excellent opportunity to make anecdotal observations reflecting on how well students are working within their groups. An observational checklist can be used by the teachers to record each student's ability to communicate positively, take responsibility, contribute to the task, and work cooperatively. To reinforce positive ways of participating in a discussion, teachers can record authentic language used by students in the room. These anonymous responses can later be shared with the class, with a teacher asking students to notice how successful these responses are in facilitating communication. Searching for new and more effective ways to communicate with others, as well as making these explicit, is ongoing.

2. Three-Dimensional Poetry

For many, the opportunity to construct a concrete representation of a poem is a very motivating experience.

One of the many ways to engage students in thinking about poetry is to have them interpret a poem and represent their understanding of its meaning in a three-dimensional form. Moving beyond language and discussion allows students with stronger visual-spatial skills to show their understanding of a poem. In choosing a way to concretely show an audience their understanding of a poem, students need to become well familiar with the text and to work out a viable interpretation. The skills they learn in the poetry discussion groups will help the students focus on imagery within the poem, identify poetic devices that the poet has used within the poem, and determine the poem's theme.

While it is useful to discuss examples and have students work together to talk about and share ideas for possible representations, we want them to read lots of poetry so that each student will find something appealing.

During their search to find a suitable poem with a theme that can be represented in a visual format, students read a great variety of poetry. They may choose one of the poems they have written or they may choose a poem from any source, as long as the poet is credited. The task is to think of a way to show the theme or meaning of the poem in a visual way to an audience. A rich and varied selection of poetry should be provided to assist the students in finding a poem that interests them.

This is the process that the students follow to create three-dimensional poetry:

- Each student selects a poem whose theme or message can be represented visually.
- The criteria for evaluation are shared with the students.
- Each student decides how to effectively display the poem and what materials will be used. Examples include mobiles, clay or wood models, origami, dioramas, hand-sewn items, multimedia displays, paintings, collages, and found objects.
- Students complete a plan for the design of the representation, including a list of the materials they will use.
- Class time is provided so that students can construct their representations within a social context.

Evaluation

Using anecdotal comments, information is collected on how well students problem-solve during the design process. Students are interviewed individually about how their representation fits the theme or message about the poem that they want to express.

The final component of this assignment is a recitation of the poem for the rest of the class. Doing this requires students to commit their poem to memory so that they can recite it confidently. Following the recitation, each student displays his or her three-dimensional representation, tells how it fits the theme of the poem, and explains the aspect of the project that resulted in a personal learning experience.

Both sets of criteria are scored on a four-point scale:

4 Moves beyond all the criteria
3 Meets all the criteria
2 Meets some of the criteria; usually has difficulty in defending the theme
1 Meets few of the criteria

This information is valuable when it comes time to write the English Language Arts portion of the report card for each student. From this activity, we have collected information about comprehension of a poem, about solving problems, and about students' ability to express themselves both in the physical representation of the poem as well as orally in front of the class. We have also gained a personal reflection about their learning.

3. Architectural Tours

All of our communities have unique architecture that is often overlooked in our daily lives. Investigating local architectural design helps students learn about the history of their community. This is highly motivating for students, as it takes them out of the classroom, helps nurture keen powers of observation, and teaches them about building design. These experiences can become the catalyst for writing free verse poetry.

Initially, the teacher gathers information about a local historic building. In one case, we studied Aberthau, a house in Vancouver whose name means "a place filled with light." Prior to arriving with the students, we toured the house,

---

We value the opportunity for students to interact and problem-solve together as the projects progress.

Project Criteria
- A theme is identified.
- A three-dimensional representation effectively displays the theme.
- The theme is supported with text evidence from the poem.

Oral Presentation Criteria
- Voice quality that serves to maintain audience interest through variations in volume and intonation
- Expression through gesture
- Eye contact with audience
- Explanation of how well the project expresses the poem in terms of its use of materials, format, and representation of the theme

The authors acknowledge the contribution of the late Jan Wells, a well-known Vancouver teacher and author. Jan worked with Catherine on the Aberthau sequence. We also thank Richmond teacher Tina Pali for her help with the Free Verse Evaluation Sheet.

Using information and unique stories, we helped to build a historical context of the house for the students.

made quick sketches of several architectural details in the house, and identified the architects as Samuel Maclure and Cecil Fox. These names then led us to the library to locate books and online sources about their architectural style and other buildings in the area.

For the tour with our students, we selected six features of the house to focus upon. In this case, we included the porte-cochère, the stained-glass and mullioned windows, the mock half-timbering, the newel posts, the parquet flooring, and the fireplace in the sitting room. Research was essential so that, when we guided students through the building, each of these features became alive with architectural information and unique stories.

As we planned the tour we considered what questions we could ask the students to enable them to discover why the house was designed as it was. For example, on the tour we asked students to consider why the porte-cochère, a covered entry porch for people entering or leaving vehicles, was incorporated as a design feature. This prompted a lively discussion about the kinds of vehicles, mainly horse-drawn carriages, that were the mode of transportation at the time the house was built. The students also noted that the amount of rainfall in Vancouver and the resulting mud made the porte-cochère a must in terms of functional design — a fact that was undoubtedly important to the women of the era, since they wore long gowns!

The lesson proceeded as follows:

- At each of the six focus points, the students listened to a brief overview or a story about the building and why the architectural feature was important.
- As they listened, students sketched the architectural feature and wrote notes, personal reflections, or questions about what they saw or heard.
- Once the tour was complete, students sat with a partner, looked at each other's illustrations, and discussed the features of the building that they found to be most interesting.
- After rereading their notes, students worked together to write descriptive phrases from their notes and drawings.
- Students each contributed a phrase for the teacher to record at the front of the class. Here are some of the phrases our students contributed:

  > "Looking through the old stained glass is like looking back in time."
  > ". . . shimmering, shining Mother of Pearl"
  > ". . . intricate tiled patterns"
  > ". . . a multitude of fireplaces"
  > "A rainforest of wood flooring"
  > ". . . damaged by weather and time"
  > "Stained glass windows dimmed by renovations"

Students who require adaptation of this writing assignment can choose 6 to 10 phrases from the class collection, practise reading them with a teacher or with a partner, and choose an order for the phrases, thereby creating a poem.

- Students now began to write a free verse poem about a particular aspect of the house or about their overall impression of the house. To build this poem, they could use the class phrases, their own phrases, and the information contained in their notes and sketches. During the writing process, the language began to become their own.

Evaluation

After several minutes of writing the first draft of their poems, students can share their leads or beginning drafts. Together they work to develop criteria for evaluation. The Free Verse Evaluation Sheet (page 116) is based on student input. The poems below are the work of students in the intermediate grades.

Lea's poem includes sensory images associated with the sights and sounds of a dance party in Aberthau. Lea successfully incorporates architectural language specific to Aberthau (the landing, stained glass, oak and mahogany). She has clearly imagined what it would have been like to attend a dance, and her strong voice is evident in her need to escape the noisy party.

Cam's poem imagines that he is arriving at Aberthau in a carriage. Although he includes only visual references to the house and has not used any architectural language, he provides a personal reaction to the house when he imagines owning it and going through it with care.

Both students use language effectively to create their impressions of the house.

many people
milling around
dancing and strutting
through the party
I must escape the noise
I rush up the stairs
and onto the landing.
The sun, low in the sky
shines through the patterned stained glass
shined oak and polished mahogany
greet me in my retreat.

Lea

From the window
in my carriage
I can see
the biggest buildings
When I step in and see
such beauty
for a moment I think
I own the whole thing.
Then I go through
the building with care.

Cam

Free Verse Evaluation Sheet

Word Choice

- Each word is carefully chosen to create a strong image, using the senses.
- More than one of the five senses are used.
- Language specific to the architecture of the house is used.

Student Evaluation /5   *Teacher Evaluation* /5

Voice

- A personal impression of the house or some aspect of the house is developed.

Student Evaluation /3   *Teacher Evaluation* /3

Flow

- Language connects together to create an image or an idea.

Student Evaluation /3   *Teacher Evaluation* /3

Ideas and Content

- You stick to your topic.
- You help the reader learn about the house and its features.

Student Evaluation /4   *Teacher Evaluation* /4

Givens

- A draft version of your poem will be turned in to the teachers.
- A minimum of 6 and a maximum of 20 phrases are included in the poem.
- Spelling has been checked.
- Your evaluation sheet has been completed.

Student Total: /15   **Teacher Total:** /15

Pembroke Publishers © 2016 *Student Diversity*, 3rd ed., by Faye Brownlie, Catherine Feniak, Leyton Schnellert ISBN 978-1-55138-318-7

9 An Integrated Unit: Social Studies and English Language Arts

Teachers are challenged by time: to find enough of it to work with curriculum content with careful thought, to teach reading and writing to diverse groups of students, to keep current with research on effective teaching strategies, and to work on creating socially responsible citizens.

Time, time, time . . . How often we hear this lament from teachers working in intermediate and middle-years classrooms. Classroom teachers Fred Weil and Tina Pali work to address this concern. As much as they can, they co-plan. Not only does working together rekindle their energy and spark new ideas, but they find that the collaboration improves their effectiveness as they pool their resources, their talents, and their passions. They work to teach reading and writing within a content area while threading through the content a theme of social responsibility.

Fred and Tina both teach combined Grades 6/7 classes. Their classes are similar to those of many teachers. They teach in an inclusive school where all students are enrolled in the regular classroom. The classes have many ELL students, students representing a wide range of ability, several students on individual education plans, and several students for whom behavior is an issue. All students are expected to participate and learn. They are supported in their learning as much as possible, although in-class learning resource support was not available at the time of this unit.

Curriculum Content: Children's Rights

The unit on children's rights was planned for four weeks. It was taught during Social Studies and English Language Arts.

The social studies content involves an examination and understanding of children's rights in different parts of the world. This content is uncovered by reading and responding to a variety of novels on the theme of children's rights, considering especially the following aspects of social responsibility:

- contributing to the classroom and the community
- solving problems in peaceful ways
- valuing diversity and defending human rights
- exercising democratic rights and responsibilities

To prepare, Fred and Tina read a wide selection of novels that connected to the theme of children's rights and that would address the range of reading interests and abilities in their classes. They also chose a variety of picture books that connected to the theme and would be used to model each assignment and to build background knowledge. These books would be available for all students to reread, but prove especially pertinent for several significantly less-able readers, who found many of the novels challenging. A new open-ended task was modeled each week of the project.

Bibliography for Children's Rights Project

Easier Titles

Haddix, Margaret Peterson. *Among the Hidden* (Shadow Children #1). New York: Aladdin, 2000.

Jordan-Fenton, Christy. *Fatty Legs: A True Story.* Toronto: Annick, 2010.

Kidd, Diana. *Onion Tears.* New York: Harper Trophy, 1993.

Laird, Elizabeth. *Secret Friends.* London: Hodder Children's Books, 1996.

Lowry, Lois. *Number the Stars.* New York: Yearling, 1990.

Velchin, Eugene. *Breaking Stalin's Nose.* New York: Henry Holt, 2011.

Whelan, Gloria. *Goodbye Vietnam.* New York: Knopf, 1992.

Williams, Laura. *Behind the Bedroom Wall.* Minneapolis: Milkweed, 1996.

Novels in Free Verse Poetry

Applegate, Katherine. *Home of the Brave.* New York: Square Fish, 2008.

Fullerton, Alma. *Libertad.* Markham: Fitzhenry & Whiteside, 2008.

Lai, Thanhha. *Inside Out and Back Again.* New York: HarperCollins, 2011.

Graphic Novels

Bell, Cece. *El Deafo.* New York: Amulet Books, 2014.

Brown, Dinah. *Who Is Malala Yousafzai?* [illustrated by Andrew Thomson]. New York: Penguin Random House, 2014.

Chikwanine, Michel, and Jessica Dee Humphreys. *Child Soldier: When Boys and Girls Are Used in War* [illustrated by Claudia Dávila]. Toronto: Kids Can Press, 2015.

Jamieson, Victoria. *Roller Girl.* New York: Dial Books for Young Readers, 2015.

Laird, Elizabeth. 2016. *Oranges in No Man's Land.* London: Macmillan Children's Books.

McCoola, Marika. *Baba Yaga's Assistant* [illustrated by Emily Carroll]. Somerville, MA: Candlewick Press, 2015.

Robertson, David. *7 Generations: A Plains Cree Saga* [illustrated by Scott B. Henderson]. Winnipeg, MB: HighWater Press, 2013.

Good Reads

Abbott, Tony. *Firegirl.* New York: Little, Brown, 2006.

Applegate, Katherine. *The One and Only Ivan.* New York: HarperCollins, 2012.

Chang, Ying. *Revolution Is Not a Dinner Party.* New York: Henry Holt, 2008.

D'Adamo, Francesco. *Iqbal.* New York: Atheneum Books for Young Readers, 2001.

Draper, Sharon. *Out of My Mind.* New York: Atheneum Books for Young Readers, 2010.

Ellis, Deborah. *The Breadwinner.* Toronto: Groundwood Books, 2001 [first in a trilogy including *Parvana's Journey* and *Mud City*].

———. *Parvana's Journey.* Toronto: Groundwood Books, 2003.

———. *The Heaven Shop.* Markham: Fitzhenry & Whiteside, 2004.

———. *Mud City.* Toronto: Groundwood Books, 2004.

Ho, Minfong. *The Clay Marble.* New York: Farrar, Straus and Giroux, 2003.

Laird, Elizabeth. *The Garbage King.* London: Macmillan Children's Books, 2003.

Victoria Jamieson's debut graphic novel, *Roller Girl,* earned a Newbery Honor Award.

A short film text set on the theme of bullying can be found at http://www.edutopia.org/blog/film-festival-bullying-prevention-upstanders.

Lord, Cynthia. *Rules*. New York: Scholastic, 2006.

Mikaelsen, Ben. *Petey*. New York: Hyperion, 1998.

Mulligan, Andy. *Trash*. Oxford: David Fickling Books, 2010.

Naidoo, Beverley. *No Turning Back*. New York: Harper Trophy, 1999.

Nielsen, Susin. *Word Nerd*. Toronto: Tundra, 2008.

———. *The Reluctant Journey of Henry K. Larsen*. Toronto: Tundra, 2012.

———. *We Are All Made of Molecules*. Toronto: Tundra, 2015.

Nye, Naomi Shihab. *Habibi*. New York: Simon Pulse, 1999.

Palacio, R. J. *Wonder*. New York: Knopf, 2012.

Park, Linda Sue. *A Single Shard*. New York: Yearling, 2001.

Sterling, Shirley. *My Name Is Seepeetza*. Vancouver: Douglas & McIntyre, 1992.

Van Draanen, Wendelin. *The Running Dream*. New York: Knopf, 2011.

Walters, Eric. *Sketches*. Toronto: Penguin Canada, 2007.

———. *Walking Home*. Toronto: Doubleday Canada, 2014.

Yousafzai, Malala, with Christina Lamb. *My Name Is Malala: The Girl Who Stood Up for Education and Was Shot by the Taliban*. Boston: Little, Brown, 2013.

Picture Books

Aliki. *Marianthe's Story: Painted Words, Spoken Memories*. New York: Greenwillow, 1998.

Bradby, Marie. *More Than Anything Else* [illustrated by Chris K. Soentpiet]. New York: Orchard, 1995.

Cutler, Jane. *The Cello of Mr. O* [illustrated by Greg Couch]. New York: Dutton Children's Books, 1999.

Heide, Florence Parry, and Judith Heide Gilliland. *Sami and the Time of the Troubles* [illustrated by Ted Lewin]. New York: Clarion Books, 1992.

Kaplan, William, and Shelley Tanaka. *One More Border: The True Story of One Family's Escape from War-Torn Europe* [illustrated by Stephen Taylor]. Vancouver: Douglas & McIntyre, 1998.

Shea, Pegi Deitz. *The Carpet Boy's Gift* [illustrated by Leane Morin]. Gardiner, ME: Tilbury House, 2006.

Wilson, Janet. *Our Rights: How Kids Are Changing the World*. Toronto: Second Story Press, 2013.

Zhang, Ange. *Red Land, Yellow River: A Story from the Cultural Revolution*. Vancouver: Douglas & McIntyre, 2004.

Beginning the Unit

Fred and Tina assigned students to pairs or groups of three, based roughly on their reading skill and on their ability to work well as partners or in groups. These partners or groups stayed together for the three- to four-week period, and agreed to read at about the same pace. The teachers quickly introduced the novels (available in twos and threes) to the students, and invited them to choose the one they and their partner(s) wanted to read.

These teachers believe in clear expectations. They also believe in involving parents as partners in the shared enterprise of their children's learning, so a unit

End-of-the-unit reflections suggested that the students would have preferred a partner change during the month and that, in choosing partners, teachers should have paid more attention to sports teams eating up a lot of certain students' time!

overview was sent home and signed by the parents. Students were expected to read at least 30 minutes a night.

Children's Rights Literature Project
Time Period: October 14 – November 14
Mr. Weil and Mrs. Pali have selected numerous books for you to choose from. We are both avid readers of children's literature and, believe it or not, have read all of them (lucky you!). We have also carefully chosen a reading partner for you. Due to uneven numbers there are a few triads. All of the books have a common theme connecting to children's rights, which we are learning about in Social Studies this term. Many of you will read 5 or 6 books easily; some may read 3. The most important thing is that you are meeting your responsibilities and putting your best effort into your assignments.

Your Responsibilities:
- Read a minimum of 30 minutes each night (including weekends). You should read more if there is no additional homework that night. We expect you to come to a consensus with your partner, as to the amount you will read.
- Be prepared for, and contribute to, partner and class discussions.
- Use the time given during class for reading, writing responses, and working on assignments wisely.
- Be cooperative with your partner. That means making sure you do the reading and come to class prepared.

Assignments
- You will be submitting small weekly assignments (e.g., double-sided response entries). More details of these will be given in class.

The marks you earn will be based on
- the degree to which you meet the given criteria for your assignments
- your participation in partner and class discussions
- your demonstration of responsibility to yourself and your partner (being focused, cooperative, and prepared)

Although we trust you and know you are responsible and cooperative, please approach your teacher if you need help in problem solving with your partner.

Please explain your responsibilities to your parents, who will sign below. Happy reading!

Mrs. Pali and Mr. Weil

Gradual Release of Responsibility: A Weekly Pattern

Gradual release:
I do.
We do.
You do.

A pattern emerged each week, beginning with modeling, to guided practice, to independent practice. Monday a picture book was used for modeling the week's strategy. On Tuesday and Wednesday, students read together and used the strategy to help draft their assignments; they handed in their draft work on Wednesday. Teachers responded to areas of needed growth on Thursday. Students worked together, then independently, and completed their assignments (based on the model) on Friday.

Monday

A picture book connecting to the theme was read. The new assignment was introduced. Criteria were established for the assignment. The teachers modeled how to complete the assignment, using the text from the picture book. The class, using the criteria, discussed how to edit the teacher's work to best achieve the criteria.

Tuesday/Wednesday

An atlas was always available in the class, and teachers began to collect background pictures to establish a context for the settings of the various novels.

Students read their books, alone or with their partner(s), and each worked on completing a draft of the assignment. These were handed in on Wednesday for feedback from the teachers. While the students worked, the teachers moved around the class, interacting with the pairs and triads of readers in mini-conferences, monitoring their progress, reading with them, checking their understanding, and scaffolding their growing understanding. One important task of the teachers was to help provide historical background for the novels.

Thursday

As the assignments were returned to the students, the teachers taught a mini-lesson on whatever need was most evident in the drafts of the students' assignments. Because the books were so compelling and this feedback so pertinent, the class discussion became highly engaging. Students were animated and involved, discussing their books and the challenges that their characters were encountering. As time permitted, students continued to read.

Friday

Students discussed, in small groups or as a class, their assignment in terms of the book they were reading and handed in the assignment for evaluation. As time permitted, they read.

Factors Associated with Successful Teaching

Several factors are key to the success of this kind of teaching:

- The curriculum is engaging and issue based.
- There is choice for students.
- All students have texts available to them that they *can* read and will *want* to read.
- Students can read at their own pace; they are not racing to keep up with the class or being held back by it.
- All students have the opportunity to engage in literate conversations with their peers.
- There is ample time for, and an expectation of, large amounts of reading.
- Teachers model the desired student performance, provide explicit criteria for meeting the expected performance, coach and offer direct feedback during the working of the assignment, and give a mark only after much learning and practising have occurred.
- Student talk abounds in the classroom.

- There are high expectations for all students and support is provided as needed for all to meet these expectations. Adaptations easily occur within the context of the regular classroom and the regular curriculum.
- Students do not flounder within a long-term assignment. First of all, there is a mandatory midweek checkup. Second, teachers can respond to a class or small-group need based on the feedback received from the student work. Third, they can also monitor those students who have difficulty organizing their time.

Sample Assignments

There are five assignments pertaining to children's rights presented here: cartoon strip panels, journal writing, writing about rights, Venn diagrams, and Readers theatre. Typically, the teachers choose three or four of them for the four-week unit.

1. Significant Events

An event in a story is significant when it changes the main character's life, growth as a person, relationship with another character, or any combination of these. The character may make a decision that has a dramatic impact on his or her life. Remember that, for this assignment, an event is not a situation, such as war or poverty, but rather something specific that causes the character to grow and change. Think about the examples we have discussed in class.

Due Date

8:45 a.m. Friday

What You Have to Do

Choose three events in your story that you think are the most significant, and explain why. Each explanation will be no longer than one paragraph. Of course, you must retell some of the story to explain your event, but we are looking for your thinking, not just retelling.

Criteria for Each Paragraph

- Knowledge of the story is demonstrated by the chosen event.
- Strong justification for choice of event is provided.
- Writing flows smoothly and makes sense.
- There is use of sophisticated language.

Format

Use the paper size you need to show the events and paragraphs. One, and only one, of your events will be illustrated in the form of a cartoon: with two or three panels and thinking and talking bubbles as needed, show what is important to the character(s) in the situation. You will need a paragraph to go with the cartoon.

How You Will Earn Your Marks

Paragraphs: 5 marks each; total of 15 marks
Cartoon: 3 marks
Overall Presentation, Neatness, Conventions: 3 marks

Other

- Naturally, you will talk with your partner about significant events, but this is an individual project and we do not expect your projects to be the same.
- You will be required to have your drafts at school for us to check your progress on Wednesday.
- Some students will be doing an adapted assignment and will be approached individually by their teachers.
- ELL students are expected to schedule a teacher conference on grammar before the due date.

A student has identified three key events in the life of Petey, title character of Ben Mikaelsen's novel about someone with cerebral palsy: gaining a close friend, a champion, and someone who wants him as a grandfather.

~Petey~   By Nicole

1) Petey meets Calvin pg.43
    I think that is important because Petey becomes (and has) a friend. Petey finally has someone to talk (well at least attempt) to and relate to. Calvin plays a important role in Petey's life, a friend a brother, and family. They spend all there time together and Calvin is the only one who can understand Petey's "Aaoo's" and "Aaee's," the only one who tries to figure out what's going on in Petey's mind, the only one to be his friend.

2) Petey meets Trevor (Trevor sticks up for Petey) pg.147
    When Trevor sees three boys picking on an old man (Petey) he sticks up for him and tries to tell the boys to "knock it off!" It seems to me that Trevor was unsure of what he was doing and thought twice before making a difference. Trevor was taking a big risk, he knew the boys would think differently about him, but that's what Petey likes about him, his courage and his friendliness.

3)Petey becomes a Grandfather pg.277
    It really touches me when Trevor asks Petey to be his Grandfather. I think it meant a lot to Petey because he was very ill at the time and for someone so young to understand him, takes courage, care and understanding. I think Trevor is very mature for his age, befriending a crippled old man would be overwhelming and almost "scary" for someone so young. Petey must of felt so loved when Trevor proposed the question "Will you be my Grandfather?" Petey must feel like a real "Grandpa."

2. Rights of the Child

The 10 rights of the child according to the United Nations are listed on your information sheet [see The 10 Rights on page 130]. These are rights that many nations agree that all children should have. In your novel, your character(s) will be denied some of these rights. As you and your partner are reading, search for evidence of what rights are being denied.

Due Date

8:45 a.m. Friday

What You Have to Do

Choose three of the children's rights that your character does not enjoy. For each right, give specific evidence from your novel that proves the character is being denied that right.

Criteria

- At least three examples of denied children's rights are identified.
- Specific evidence from the story demonstrates how each right is denied.
- Information is presented in a clear, organized, and interesting way.

Format

- Use 8.5" by 11" paper.
- Choose any format you wish, provided you meet the criteria.

How You Will Earn Your Marks

Rights and evidence — detailed evidence from the story to show the character has at least three children's rights denied: 10 marks
Presentation — organized, categorized presentation of information: 3 marks
Conventions — few errors, which do not interfere with meaning: 2 marks

The same four points listed under "Other" on page 123 apply to this partner activity, too.

Here is how one student identified and discussed three rights that an Indigenous Canadian girl attending a residential school in the 1950s had been denied.

My Name Is Seepeetza

Seepeetza didn't have
The Right to her Own Culture

It was in the law that the Indians couldn't practice their own religion. The nuns taught them in school and made them practice the Catholic religion. The Indian children had to learn English; some of them even forgot how to speak their native language. The nuns also had them change their Indian names to Catholic names.

Seepeetza didn't have
The Right to Protection from Harm

The nuns used the strap and other awful devices for discipline. It doesn't do anything except make all the kids that get beat, dislike the nuns and wish that they didn't have to go to that school.

Seepeetza didn't have
The Right of Non Discrimination

She was discriminated against for being an Indian. She had to change her Indian name to a Catholic name, which was Martha. She was not allowed to be taught by Indians, but was forced to travel far away to learn the Catholic ways instead of her Indian traditions. I think the nuns should treat Indians like they treat themselves, because the Indians are people just like the nuns, the only thing that is different between them is their race, and that should have nothing to do with whether or not they like each other.

Clint

3. Double-Entry Response Journals

Ten double-entry response journal prompts are given in line-master form on page 126.

There are 10 different double-entry response journal prompts. Essentially, the question on the left side of the page will require you to think specifically about text-based information. The question on the right side of the page will require you to use this text information to think critically, make inferences, respond personally, or offer supported reactions and opinions.

Due Date

8:45 a.m. Friday

What You Have to Do

Choose 4 of the 10 response journal prompts that will best demonstrate your understanding of the novel. Assume that to respond well to each prompt on the right side of the page will require much writing, likely about a page.

Criteria/Marks

- Left-side questions — 4 well-chosen and accurately documented responses (with specific text references): 2 marks each; total of 8 marks
- Right-side questions — sophisticated responses that may contain personal connections (between books or between the book and your life), supported reactions and opinions, inferential thinking, and critical thinking: 4 marks each; total of 16 marks
- Writing — connected thoughts, sophisticated language: 3 marks
- Conventions — any errors in spelling and grammar not interfering with meaning: 2 marks

4. Triple Venn Diagram

A Venn diagram is a graphic organizer that helps organize your thinking while you compare and contrast three characters from three different books you have read.

Due Date

8:45 a.m. Friday

Ten Double-Entry Journal Response Prompts

1. What is the setting of your novel?

1. Describe the setting of the novel in terms of landscape, climate, time period, human environment and the like. How does the main character fit into the setting? How does it compare with where you live?

2. What question do you have from reading this novel?

2. Ask your question of at least two different people. What do you learn from their responses?

3. Find a passage that is very descriptive. Write this out and sketch your image of the passage.

3. How does the author create the image of a particular setting, character, or event in this passage? Does the author use imagery or special language?

4. What is an important choice or decision that a character has to make?

4. Explain the choice, why the character makes it, and whether you think it was a wise choice.

5. What is an important relationship that a main character has with another character?

5. Explain who the relationship is with and what kind of relationship it is. Explain how the relationship develops or changes over time.

6. What inner resources does the main character use to overcome the challenges that he or she faces?

6. Explain what traits and personal strengths the main character has and give specific examples from the story of when the character demonstrates these traits.

7. How does a main character show personal growth or change over the course of the story?

7. Explain how the character experiences a positive change in personality, such as gaining greater resilience, understanding, or caring for others.

8. Is there an artifact or object that has special significance in your story?

8. Explain why a particular object is important in the story. Does the author use that object as a symbol of some kind?

9. What is the meaning of the title?

9. Explain the title of the story. You might comment on whether you think it is well chosen or not. Would you have chosen a different title for the story?

10. Choose an event that you found particularly frightening or hopeful. Retell this event.

10. Explain why the event was particularly frightening or hopeful to you. Be sure to make personal connections and support your opinion with specific detail.

Pembroke Publishers © 2016 *Student Diversity*, 3rd ed., by Faye Brownlie, Catherine Feniak, Leyton Schnellert ISBN 978-1-55138-318-7

What You Have to Do

Compare and contrast three characters from the three books you have read in the form of a Venn diagram. Describe, in point form, similarities and differences between your three characters. If you have read only two books, you can be the third character. Use the areas where the circles overlap to show similarities, and the rest of the circle to show differences.

Criteria

- Important character traits
- Family information
- The setting or situation your character is in (e.g., Germany in World War II)
- The children's rights your character is being denied
- Any other information that is relevant to your novel

Format

- Label each circle with your character name and the novel title.
- Use an 11" by 14" or 11" by 17" piece of paper so you have lots of room for neat printing.
- If you are able to do Venn diagrams on your computer, go for it!

How You Will Earn Your Marks

- Selection of a range of important similarities and differences in your characters on the basis of
  - character traits
  - family information
  - setting or situation
  - children's rights that are being denied
  - other information relevant to your novel

15 possible marks

- Overall presentation, including
  - conventions such as spelling and capitalization
  - neatness
  - use of titles and headings
  - design and illustrations that are related to your novels

5 possible marks

5. Readers Theatre

Readers theatre is an opportunity for you and your partner to represent and share an important event from a book you have both read.

Due Date

Friday, class time

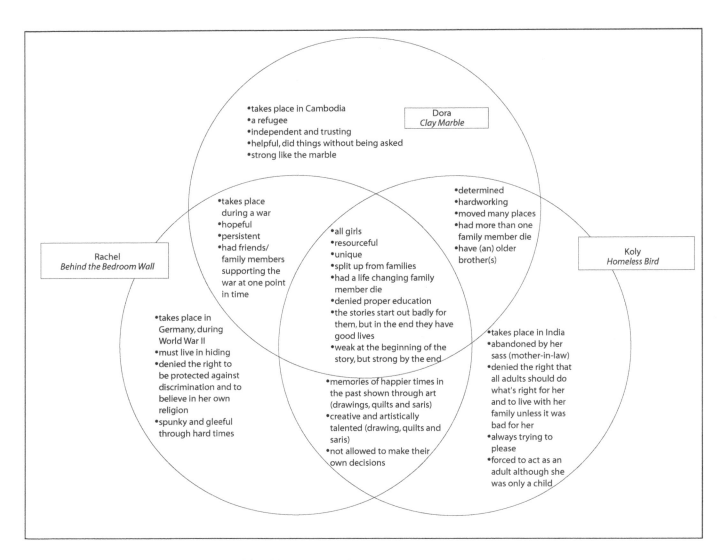

The following text appears within the Venn diagram:

Dora
Clay Marble

•takes place in Cambodia
•a refugee
•independent and trusting
•helpful, did things without being asked
•strong like the marble

Rachel
Behind the Bedroom Wall

•takes place during a war
•hopeful
•persistent
•had friends/ family members supporting the war at one point in time

•determined
•hardworking
•moved many places
•had more than one family member die
•have (an) older brother(s)

Koly
Homeless Bird

•all girls
•resourceful
•unique
•split up from families
•had a life changing family member die
•denied proper education
•the stories start out badly for them, but in the end they have good lives
•weak at the beginning of the story, but strong by the end

•takes place in Germany, during World War II
•must live in hiding
•denied the right to be protected against discrimination and to believe in her own religion
•spunky and gleeful through hard times

•memories of happier times in the past shown through art (drawings, quilts and saris)
•creative and artistically talented (drawing, quilts and saris)
•not allowed to make their own decisions

•takes place in India
•abandoned by her sass (mother-in-law)
•denied the right that all adults should do what's right for her and to live with her family unless it was bad for her
•always trying to please
•forced to act as an adult although she was only a child

For her Venn diagram, the student has provided detailed and complete comparative information about each of her three main characters. She has found similarities among the three characters and between the characters in twos; she has also described each setting and given an example of a denied children's right. Clearly, the student has understood and reflected on her reading.

What You Have to Do

Choose a passage from the novel with a lot of dialogue or a particularly significant event in the novel, and create a dialogue for it. Together you and your partner will write the dialogue, practise performing it, and then present it to the class.

Criteria/Marks

- Script
  - introduction to the passage, 3 marks
  - script choice, 2 marks
  - script content, 3 marks

- Performance (for each presenter)
  - volume, 4 marks
  - expression, 4 marks
  - stayed in role, 2 marks

- Peer and self-evaluation: How did you and your partner(s) contribute to this activity? Make a circle graph to show your contributions and explain your thinking.

> Readers Theatre
> Flight of the Doves by Walter Macken
> Judge, Derval – Chase
> Finn, Narrator, Uncle Toby – Gerry
>
> Introduction: Our story is called "Flight of the Doves" and it takes place in England and Ireland. Finn and Derval are brother and sister at ages 12 and 7. Finn and Derval wanted to escape their vicious uncle Toby and went to Ireland where their loving granny and uncle RC and uncle Paddy live. They make it to their destination but they also had many cops and citizens trying to get them back to uncle Toby. We picked the scene where Finn and Derval were in granny's house and they are being questioned by the judge. Suddenly, Derval says something shocking and the judge tries to find the truth. We picked this scene because it really was powerful, the way Derval had the courage to speak up the truth and say such a thing.

The students have provided the context for their script and developed a script based on a scene that they found powerful. They have identified Finn as being courageous in saying that he would, indeed, run away again, taking Derval with him. They have also chosen a scene that highlights Finn's humility. Their work demonstrates compassion for the characters and an understanding of the novel.

> JUDGE: Do you feel that you have done a great deed, running away from home, crossing the sea, making hares out of police, and triumphantly arriving at your destination?
> FINN: Oh no.
> JUDGE: But you should, it was a remarkable thing to do.
> FINN: But I didn't do it.
> JUDGE: What do you mean?
> FINN: Well, it was all the other people, all the people that helped us. Poll, Tom, Mickser, Moses and Michael. If it wasn't for them we would have been caught long ago.
> JUDGE: I see. So you hadn't much to do with it.
> FINN: Oh no.
> JUDGE: I see. If you are returned to your uncle Toby, what would you do, Finn?
> FINN: I would run away the first chance I got.
> JUDGE: Would you bring Derval?
> FINN: Yes.
> JUDGE: Why?

Cross-Curricular Team Benefits

Tina and Fred have found that co-planning and co-teaching, when possible, has enriched and energized their teaching. They have also found that one of the ways to address the ever-present issue of finding time to work with curriculum is to plan cross-curricular and integrated units. The extensive reading that their students engaged in deepened their understanding of the big ideas of the Social Studies curriculum, and as students gained more content knowledge, they read with greater understanding and engagement. The framework Fred and Tina used in this unit helped provide them with time to meet with students individually and in twos and threes, guiding and extending student learning in individually appropriate ways, governed by the overarching and inclusive goals of the unit.

The 10 Rights

1. **Education — our right to an education**
   We have the right to education. Governments have the responsibility to guarantee that primary education is compulsory and free of charge, and to take steps so that we all have equal access to secondary and higher education. The discipline used in our schools must not go against our human dignity. Our education should help us develop our own personalities and abilities; prepare us to become responsible members of a free society; and develop respect for our parents or guardians, for human rights, for the environment, and for cultural and national values.

2. **Family — our right to have family to care for us**
   We have the right to live with our parents unless this is against our best interests, and to be reunited with our families across international borders. Both of our parents are responsible for our upbringing; governments must respect this and support our parents in bringing us up. Our right to care also means that if we are deprived of a family environment, we have the right to special protection, are entitled to alternative care that respects our background, and have the right to a regular review of that care. In the case of adoption, our best interests must be considered.

3. **Food and Shelter — our right to food and shelter**
   We have the right to a decent standard of living for our physical, mental, spiritual, moral, and social well-being, and we have the right to benefit from social security, including social insurance. Those of us who have a disability have the right to special care, education, and training.

4. **Health — our right to a safe environment and healthy life**
   Governments must do all possible to make sure that children survive and develop. We have the right to the best possible level of health care available, and to clean air and water.

5. **Name and Nationality — our right to have a name and acquire a nationality**
   We have the right to be given a name, to acquire a nationality and, whenever possible, to know and to be cared for by our parents. Governments have an obligation to protect our identity, name, nationality, and family ties.

6. **Non-discrimination — our right to be treated fairly without discrimination**
   All rights apply to all children, no matter who we are or where we live.

7. **Own Cultures — our right to our own cultures**
   We have the right to enjoy and practise our own cultures, languages, and religions, especially if we belong to a minority or Indigenous population.

8. **Protection from Harm — our right to protection from harmful acts**
   We have the right to be protected from abuse, neglect, torture, sexual exploitation, the use and distribution of drugs, and abduction. We have the right to be protected from having to participate in work that threatens our health, education, or development. We have the right to special protection in times of war and fair treatment if arrested. Governments must take steps to prevent harm and exploitation and to provide treatment for those who have been abused or exploited, have been in conflict with the law, or have experienced armed conflict or torture. Governments must set minimum ages for employment and regulate working conditions.

9. **Rest and Play — our right to rest and play**
   We have the right to rest, leisure, play, and participation in cultural and artistic activities.

10. **Thought and Opinions — our right to have freedom of thought and share our opinions**
    We have the right to express our views and opinions and to have these opinions listened to in matters that affect us. We have the right to freedom of thought, conscience, and religion, the freedom to receive information from many sources, the freedom to meet with others and to join or start our own associations, and the freedom from governmental invasions of our privacy.

Pembroke Publishers © 2016 *Student Diversity*, 3rd ed., by Faye Brownlie, Catherine Feniak, Leyton Schnellert ISBN 978-1-55138-318-7

10 Science: Multiple Intelligences at Work

We believe it is important to broaden the means by which students can communicate scientific knowledge. In seeking a framework to do this, we have made practical use of Howard Gardner's theory of multiple intelligences as presented in his 2002 book, *Intelligence Reframed: Multiple Intelligences for the Twenty-First Century*.

Catherine, then a classroom teacher, co-planned the "living things" portion of the science curriculum for her class of intermediate students with the learning resource teacher and teacher-librarian. They worked together to enhance the students' ability to interpret the local environment and to conduct an inquiry to find answers to their questions. The activities in this unit were designed to allow students to build their knowledge about a local ecosystem and then represent and communicate their understanding of that part of the natural world in a variety of ways consistent with the theory of multiple intelligences. The activities enabled English language learners to build their understanding through a variety of experiences — not just reading and writing. They opened up opportunities for students who thrive on open-ended exploration — no ceiling was placed on their participation. They also recognized that students who are challenged academically can prove to be powerful learners when provided with new ways to demonstrate their understanding.

Integrating the Multiple Intelligences for Learning

In Howard Gardner's multiple intelligences theory, there are eight key ways of acquiring new learning and of demonstrating that learning. Each person has all of the intelligences and a personal profile reflecting more strength in some of the intelligences than in others. Intelligences can be nurtured and developed throughout life. They are identified as follows:

- verbal-linguistic — "word smart," able to analyze information and express ideas in written and oral language
- logical-mathematical — "number smart," able to solve mathematical problems and complete number activities
- visual-spatial — "picture smart," good at map reading and obtaining information from graphics
- musical — "music smart," can make meaning from a variety of sounds
- bodily-kinesthetic — "body smart," can use the body creatively and in solving problems
- naturalist — "nature smart," can identify and distinguish plants, animals, and weather patterns
- interpersonal — "people smart," able to recognize the moods, motivations, and intentions of others
- intrapersonal — "myself smart," self-understanding of personal moods, motivations, and intentions

The concepts we chose to teach in this ecology unit included the following terms:

herbivore, omnivore, carnivore, decomposer, food web, food chain, ecosystem, biogeoclimatic zone, predator, prey, biodiversity, interdependent, life cycle, producer, consumer, and *photosynthesis.*

People Search Sample

Find someone who

knows the name of a carnivore from a famous movie or fairytale
_____
_____
Signature

During our planning it became clear that, to reach the goal of teaching students to communicate scientifically, we needed to provide opportunities for the students to develop a repertoire of skills that enabled them to integrate these intelligences.

We designed a variety of lessons that involved students in discovering more about the important concepts through small-group activities:

- having a People Search at the beginning of the unit to determine the level of understanding that the students possessed about these ecological concepts, for example, prompting students to find someone who "can name a decomposer that is eaten in salads" (see People Search: Science on page 137)
- making three-column notes when watching a video or reading non-fiction texts,

Word and Its Meaning	**Details**	**Drawing**

then working together to ensure that all group members have accurately recorded facts, details, and drawings for each of the concepts (see Three-Column Notes on page 138)

- making personal connections, text–media connections, and connections to the world around them when students discussed these concepts in small as well as large groups

Things I know and things about me	Things I've read or seen in movies or on TV	Connections to the world and big ideas

- showing a food web or life cycle using movement or drama and music
- obtaining information through multi-source and multi-level resources, including picture books, magazines, non-fiction books, pamphlets, video, and websites (For intermediate students, the selection of books included those read by students in Grades 3 through 8.)

Once the students had gained an understanding of these concepts, a group field trip was planned to develop the students' observational skills and their naturalist and bodily-kinesthetic intelligences in a forest setting. Park naturalists designed the outdoor activities so that these concepts would come alive for the students. The naturalists reinforced the vocabulary that had been used throughout the unit, demonstrating to the students how biologists use these concepts when communicating with others.

Evaluation: Multiple Representations of Understanding

We wanted to assess how well group members worked together to achieve their goal of communicating in a scientific way, and we also wanted to know how well individual students could communicate their knowledge.

To deepen the students' understanding, we designed our summative assessment so that they could make connections between the concepts taught in the unit and a local ecosystem. The evaluation had to be both group and individual.

Here are the steps we followed:

1. Students were placed in heterogeneous groups. From a list of local ecosystems — seashore, pond, estuary, river, forest, marsh, or creek — each group chose one for their project.

2. The students arranged a field study so that they could visit the ecosystem together. Observations of the area were made in a variety of ways, including life lists, photographs, video recordings, observational notes, and drawings.

3. Each student in the group would become an expert by learning in-depth about one organism in the ecosystem. Using an essay outline (see page 134), each student wrote about the chosen organism.

4. The art teacher showed students techniques for constructing a diorama.

5. Each group constructed a diorama, using non-living materials to show interdependence and ways that insects, birds, plants, reptiles, and animals living in the ecosystem respond to their environment. The diorama had to include the organisms researched by each group member and also a clearly labeled food web.

Essential criteria included the following:
- The diorama includes a clearly labeled food web for at least one organism in the ecosystem.
- The diorama shows an example of interdependence between a plant and animal in the ecosystem.

Important Components for Criteria
Essay:
- Accurate use of scientific vocabulary
- Consistent use of bibliography format
- All paragraph subtopics included
- Conventions of writing

Diorama:
- Realistic representation of the ecosystem
- Food web clearly shown
- Overall impact of the diorama
- Organisms represented in the diorama

Evaluation of the essays and dioramas was completed using the following process:

- The students brainstormed all the important components of the dioramas and of the essays.
- The teachers helped the students to organize the criteria into categories for ease of evaluation. If needed, we added criteria and explained to the students why these were important to include.
- The criteria and rating scale were posted, and the teams refined their dioramas against these criteria before moving to the team evaluation process.
- During the team evaluation process, students continued to work in the same groups. Each group was given a different component of the project to evaluate.
- Members of each group worked together to arrive at a consensus before assigning a score out of 5 for the project component they were evaluating.
- The teachers reviewed the marks assigned by the student teams.
- The essays were read by the teachers and evaluated using the following scale:
  5 The student has exceeded the expectations, demonstrating insight and creativity.
  4 The student has successfully met all of the criteria.
  3 The student has met most of the criteria.
  2 The student has met only some of the criteria.
  1 The task was inappropriate for the student at this time.

Throughout this process, students were able to read and see the projects produced by their peers in the class. When they saw the range of ways to complete the project, they gained new ideas for tackling future assignments.

The evaluation process gave students a chance to witness how a subjective evaluation is completed. Some of the groups' debates on how to score particular projects were very illuminating for us as teachers. In most cases, it was evident that the students valued the same things that we did when evaluating their work. The students had fun, experienced much success, learned a lot of science, and moved their learning outside the traditional boundaries of the classroom.

Essay Outline: Interdependence Project

Use the following format as a guide for the essay about the organism you chose for your part of the Interdependence Project.

Paragraph 1

- Provide a topic sentence that introduces the essay subject.
- Identify the organism that has been studied.
- Include the Latin and common names (if both can be found).
- Tell whether your organism is a predator or prey.

Paragraph 2

- Identify the location of the organism.
- Describe the ecosystem, niche, climate, and biogeoclimatic zone where your organism lives and finds shelter.
- Describe the other organisms that live in this ecosystem.

Paragraph 3

- Explain how the organism fits into the food web.
- Describe and provide evidence of the organism as a herbivore, carnivore, or omnivore.
- Explain how the organism is interdependent with other organisms.

Paragraph 4

- Describe changes in the ecosystem that have occurred or are still occurring.
- Describe problems that this organism has to face.
- Describe the adaptations, if any, the organism has made to survive.

Paragraph 5

- Summarize the main ideas of your essay.
- Describe what needs to be done to protect this organism.
- Describe what must be done to protect the ecosystem where it lives.
- Leave the readers with an idea of something that they could do to assist in protecting the biodiversity in our local ecosystems.

Bibliography

Please include all of the resources you used, and follow the bibliography format outlined by the teacher librarian.

Pembroke Publishers © 2016 *Student Diversity*, 3rd ed., by Faye Brownlie, Catherine Feniak, Leyton Schnellert ISBN 978-1-55138-318-7

The following two essays are samples of how all students could participate with success in this unit.

Raccoon

Have you ever shooed away a raccoon eating your garbage? Next time that you see one, stop and watch it for awhile. You will see that raccoons are very misunderstood. Raccoons are very playful creatures and they are not trying to upset humans. The fact that they have adapted to city life and are not afraid of humans is not their fault at all. Raccoons are consumers. They eat other things. So why are they living in the center of the city? This and much more will be answered in this report.

The raccoon is an omnivore. This means they eat a variety of different things. Some of the raccoons favorite foods are: crayfish, fish, frogs, garbage, mice and squirrels. The raccoon also eats things that are already dead and some plants. Because most things raccoons eat live in the water, they like to live where there is fresh water nearby. There is not a lot of things that eat raccoons but since they live near the city, the raccoon population is kept down by people in cars and the fact that they are not protected. Some things that do eat raccoons are cougars, bears, wolves and other big cats. Most of these animals prefer to eat the babies.

The raccoon lives in the forest. They live in cavities in trees, ditches in the ground and other sheltered areas. Raccoons are not very picky about their location but since they like to live near water, they usually don't live very high up in the mountains. They also can't survive in very, very cold climates like the Yukon. Most raccoons don't care about what kind of forests they live in as long as they have all of the above. This is probably why they like Vancouver so much. The fact is, they are not living in the city, we are living in the forest. If you think about it, raccoons have probably been living in Vancouver for hundreds of years. Then we decided to build our city right in the middle of the forest. For example, the North shore mountains, Stanley Park and Pacific Spirit Park were all here before us and were all homes for raccoons. Now raccoons have decided to live in city parks because we took down so much of their habitat.

A raccoon's life cycle is very simple. They are considered babies for around two years. For the first year, they stay in their homes almost all of the time. They live on their mothers' milk for only about six months. When they are two years old, they can leave their homes but they usually stay close to their mothers for the first month. Baby raccoons are very playful and curious. This is how most baby raccoons are hurt or killed. They sometimes might wander on to a busy road without their mothers seeing and end up badly injured. Raccoons in zoos can live up to about fifteen years but in the wild they live about only twelve years because of the amount of dangers. Some drastic changes that have happened in the raccoons ecosystem are clear cutting, highways and toxic garbage. Raccoons are now used to traffic and people but they don't always remember about cars when they are crossing the road. They have become so used to roads being there that they don't consider them being a threat. One major change to the ecosystem is that the forest is being cut down rapidly. This is why raccoons are not living in parks, riverbeds and even people's backyards. Another threat to raccoons is that if people throw away some fish and toxic garbage in the same bag, the raccoons might eat the poison and get sick or die.

So next time you see a raccoon, watch it and learn. Try to be careful not to throw away toxins and food in the same bag and learn to care about the forest. We protect our homes from burglars but raccoons can't protect the forest against us.

Lindsay

Both Lindsay and Byron have successfully followed the essay outline to guide them in including specific information about raccoons and cat tails. They have included information about the life cycle and habitats of their organisms. Lindsay has applied the scientific vocabulary she learned to correctly use the terms *consumer* and *omnivore*, and Byron included the Latin name for the cat tail. Their concluding paragraphs outline the changes to the ecosystems that the raccoon and cat tails must adapt to in order to survive. They also provide recommendations for what needs to be done in order to protect raccoons and cat tail plants.

Cat Tails

The cat tail has two names — one is called a cat tail and the other name is bull rush. Some people and a lot of books call it a cat tail because at the end of the brown round part it looks like it has a tail. The cat tails have flat leaves about an inch wide. They have a strong stem that grows high. Four quarters of the way up is a dark brown and oval shape, which is part of the cat tail. The cat tail contains pollen grains and just above it is a little tip that looks like a tail. The Latin name for cat tails is Typha Latifotia. This organism is prey for the Red Wing Black birds and the Muskrats.

This organism is located in estuaries in Vancouver and Richmond and many other places. I saw them in Terra Nova next to the river — there are thousands of them growing there. Cat tails live in many different climates including those which get snow to heat. It lives in very swampy waters, but has no shelter from rain. A lot of dead trees are in the area where they live.

The cat tails fit into the food web when Red Wing Black birds or Muskrats take the pollen for food. Then they die over the years and make better soil which the cat tails use to survive. When the snow geese come near winter they drop their droppings and that is good for the soil too. Cat tails are eaten by Herbivores because they use the soil to survive. If there was no soil or animals there would not be any cat tails.

There is less room for them to grow because people took up all the room in the beginning of Terra Nova and in other places. It is also facing pollution because you drive right up to where they are when you go for a walk. To survive, the dark brown just before the tip turns into fluff to spread to make more cat tails in years to come.

To protect the cat tails we should give them more room to grow, move them away from the pollution and we will see many more. To protect where it lives there should be not any cars around so that it can live without pollution. No one should litter because it is hard for them to live with all the garbage so throw it in the garbage bins.

Byron

Thinking Like a Scientist

Exploring Science

- Hypothesize.
- Notice.
- Wonder.
- Document.
- Explain.
- Revise one's thinking.

Repeat.

Teaching and learning science asks teachers and students to develop scientific literacy. We need to think like scientists, to hypothesize, to notice, to wonder, to document, to explain, and to revise our thinking. These competencies describe how science — and scientists — work. We learn through exploration and build our understandings by taking part in cycles of exploration. During the featured unit, our students used their verbal-linguistic, logical-mathematical, visual-spatial, naturalist, interpersonal, and intrapersonal intelligences at different times to both learn and to express their learning. We can help students develop their critical, creative, and reflective thinking in science through inquiry, investigation, and communicating with authentic audiences.

People Search: Science

Directions

Meet for short periods of time with your classmates so you can learn more about the following concepts. As you gather information, record the answer and ask the person who gave it to sign in the same box. Each box must contain the name of a different student.

Find someone who

knows the name of a carnivore from a famous movie or fairytale _____ _____ Signature	can explain what the prefix *bio* means _____ _____ Signature	can make a sketch of a local ecosystem [ ] _____ Signature
knows some of the things that a herbivore would eat _____ _____ Signature	can name a decomposer that is eaten in salads _____ _____ Signature	can explain why photosynthesis is important _____ _____ Signature
can draw and label a predator as it stalks its prey [ ] _____ Signature	can name a famous omnivore living in BC forests _____ _____ Signature	is able to guess what a biogeoclimatic zone is _____ _____ Signature

Pembroke Publishers © 2016 *Student Diversity*, 3rd ed., by Faye Brownlie, Catherine Feniak, Leyton Schnellert ISBN 978-1-55138-318-7

Three-Column Notes

Word and Its Meaning	Details	Drawing
1.	a. b. c.	
2.	a. b. c.	
3.	a. b. c.	
4.	a. b. c.	
5.	a. b. c.	

Pembroke Publishers © 2016 *Student Diversity*, 3rd ed., by Faye Brownlie, Catherine Feniak, Leyton Schnellert ISBN 978-1-55138-318-7

11 Math: Reaching All Learners in the Classroom

This chapter has been contributed by learning resource teacher Carole Fullerton.

Filled with tricks and rules to remember, mathematics has often been a subject only few could understand, let alone master; however, it need not be a four-letter word.

Ask anyone what their least favorite subject was in school and they will likely tell you it was math. The anxiety arising from having to find the one right answer and to find it quickly disenfranchised so many learners that people came to believe themselves incapable of understanding mathematics. Rigid teaching methods — a quick demo of the procedure of the day, followed by pages of practice — made math incomprehensible to most children, or at best boring and irrelevant.

Notions of diversity traditionally have not extended into the math classroom; children who did not grasp the concepts were relegated to endless drill of the basic facts. In an effort to "simplify" content, students with learning difficulties were presented with stripped-down math, numbers on the page. Rarely did they engage in rich conceptual tasks.

We are learning to re-imagine math classrooms as places where students of all abilities work together on the same problem: a rich task focused on a concept worth revisiting over time. Real math is accessible to all members of the class community and different solution methods are honored and celebrated.

Reconsidering Tasks and Lesson Structure

The work of mathematician John Van de Walle has permeated our thinking and sculpted changes about how to teach math. Van de Walle's beliefs about mathematics learning parallel our view of literacy learning. Van de Walle states that to create mathematics classes that engage all students of diverse abilities and help more students learn and enjoy mathematics, we must reconsider not just the *tasks* we present to students but the *structure* of the math lessons.

Providing Rich Tasks

Tasks are about concepts (such as "division as sharing") rather than procedures.

Math tasks best meet the needs of diverse learners when they are focused on the math concepts, involve open-ended questions, and are contextualized through the use of story problems.

Focus the tasks on the math

Rather than practising more long division questions, intermediate students might consider these questions:

- When is it appropriate to divide a remainder into fractional pieces?
- When is a remainder negligible?

- In which contexts does having a remainder change the value of the quotient?
- Can you really rent 3.6 buses to go to the Aquarium?

These questions will help students understand that when we divide there is almost always a remainder and that how we handle that remainder depends on the context of the problem.

Ask open-ended questions

Open-ended questions invite students to find multiple answers to a problem, or to solve a problem in a variety of ways.

If we ask "What is $380 \div 15$?" there is only one right answer — 25 remainder 5, or 25.3333 — and one assumed right method. Some students will find the answer effortlessly and be ready for another question quickly, while some will struggle with the algorithm, perhaps arriving at the right answer without fully understanding the question or the processes involved.

Instead we might ask: "How can you show 380 divided into 15 groups? How many different ways can you find? Show your thinking in numbers, pictures, and words." If we do so, we invite students with different strengths to draw, build, or write about their ideas. Mathematical thinking is broadened and more accessible.

Contextualize the tasks

Making connections and making sense are key.

Rather than using traditional word problems, we recommend adopting story problems. Here is an example:

> We'll be working with our little buddy class later this week to make craft stick rafts. The instructions we found show that each raft needs 15 sticks. We have gathered 380 sticks so far. Our little buddy class has 26 students. Will we have enough craft sticks to make rafts for everyone? How could you figure this out? Show your thinking in at least 2 different ways.

This context asks students to solve a division-by-grouping problem, to assess the meaning of the remainder, and to show more than one way to solve the problem. This is a rich task, one that all students in an intermediate or middle classroom can access, even if it means counting out 380 craft sticks and making groups of 15. But consider how much you could learn about your students' conceptual understanding by asking this complex question instead of presenting them with $380 \div 15$.

Structuring the Lesson Effectively

Like our literacy lessons, our math lessons are 80 minutes long. This period allows time for the stages of the lesson. Like our literacy lessons, the stages are as follows:

- before (connecting)
- during (processing)
- after (personalizing and transforming)

A typical lesson structure might go this way:

BEFORE: CONNECTING • Stage setting and connection making A question, quick problem, or reminder of previous learning	5–10 minutes

DURING: PROCESSING • Presentation of the day's task Shared exploration of the task • Student exploration and investigation of a new, connected problem	20–30 minutes
AFTER: PERSONALIZING AND TRANSFORMING • Strategy sharing and consolidation Time to compare solutions and strategies, and to share thinking • Reflecting and practice Writing or drawing to explain key learning; applying learning to new situations	10–20 minutes 20–30 minutes

Introducing Division

In this Grades 5/6 class, in just one lesson, a significant shift occurs in the students' use of precise math language and in their conceptual understanding of division. In co-planning for the lesson, the classroom teacher, Liz Nasu, has told me (learning resource teacher Carole Fullerton) that the students' understanding of place value was not strong. Together, we established the goals for the lesson:

- to introduce division in a visual, non-algorithmic way
- to address and build place-value concepts through problem solving
- to develop mathematical language (specifically around division)
- to engage all learners

Before: Connecting

Teachers Carole Fullerton and Liz Nasu set the stage for a lesson on division by having students consider what they knew about mathematical language and where it might be used. Before they presented the task of the day, they wanted students to access and share their background knowledge.

The teacher-produced text labels parts of a division equation and includes "left over" as the less formal name for remainder.

We began the lesson by generating some vocabulary around division. We put an equation on the board and asked if students could guess what the lesson of the day was going to address. They quickly guessed division and pointed out that the clues were the division sign and the *R3* for "Remainder 3." We labeled these items and prompted them to give another name for remainder.

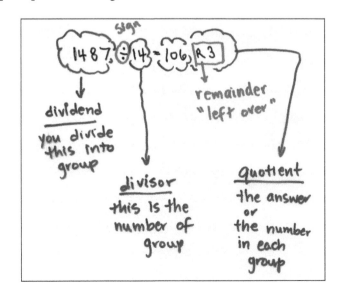

Since the specific vocabulary of division had not surfaced, we circled the other numbers in the equation. We asked the students to work in their groups to come up with the proper names for each of the terms — but also to think of a way to describe these terms to someone much younger. They worked in their groups. The mathematical language they shared and called up was rich: students made connections to prior grades, to other lessons, and to places they might find this kind of language used.

During: Processing

As it was just after Halloween, we used a related math problem. My son and I had been trick-or-treating and needed to share our 124 candies with four people. Some students used mental math and quickly shouted out that everyone should get 31 candies. Liz and I agreed, but reminded them that my son was only eight years old and would not believe this unless we could show him how we arrived at 31 as a number.

I used base-ten blocks on the Smart Board and built 124 with one flat of 100, two rods of 10, and 4 singles.

"Okay," I said, "I have the dividend 124. What should I do next?"

Cara volunteered the next step, suggesting that I break the 100 flat up into tens so I could share the pieces. I wrote her idea down in words on the Smart Board, then invited her to come up and show me how to do that. Cara traded the 100 for 10 tens and placed them on the Smart Board.

The next student, Jordan, said that I should "take the tens and make four groups." I wrote his directions on the Smart Board and had him come up and model his idea.

We continued, recording student language and movement of the manipulatives until the quotient was found. I confirmed for them that my son would believe this series of instructions: they were clear and showed how the students had arrived at 31 as the answer.

Presentation of the Day's Task

We posed the problem for the day, selecting a student from the class as the subject of the problem.

> Ji Ye has 15 sets of collector cards. All the sets have an equal number of cards. Ji Ye has 375 cards. How many collector cards are in each set?

I grabbed a pen and began a think-aloud for the problem. I told the students that, although teachers often just seem to know how to solve problems, there is a process that happens in a teacher's brain each time. "Let me share what's going on in my brain for a bit . . .," I said. I started to doodle and draw and mused:

Ji Ye has 15 sets of collector cards. Hmm. Maybe they're like hockey cards or something. *All the sets have an equal number of cards.* Oh, okay. They must all be the same brand of cards — they've all come in packages like in tens or something. *Ji Ye has 375 cards.* Whoa. That's a lot of cards. She's been collecting for a while. *How many collector cards are in each set?* Must be more than 10 in a set because 15 sets of 10 would give only 150 cards. Okay. What should I do first? Let's see. What do I know for sure?

I paused and went back to the beginning of the problem. At the students' prompting, I underlined the words *15 sets* and wrote this below the problem. I said: "That's right. There are 15 sets of cards altogether."

Next, I underlined the words *375 cards*. I labeled each of these terms, the first as the divisor and the second as the dividend. Then I said:

> Now I see that there's a question here that needs answering. It wants to know how many collector cards are in a set. I wonder how I could figure that out. I know that the dividend tells me how many cards there are altogether — and the divisor tells me how many are in a group.

I asked students to sort out which of the numbers in the problem was the dividend and which was the divisor. "What are we supposed to find?" I asked.

"The answer," said one student.

I prompted some more.

"I mean the quotient," he corrected himself. "That means we'll have to divide."

I turned to the students and told them to solve this problem in their groups. They could make use of base-ten blocks. They should record their process while they worked. They were to share the recording job so that everyone had a chance to record a stage of de-constructing the whole.

Each group was given a digital camera to photograph the stages of the process. This was a critical piece of the lesson's goals — to experience many different ways to divide and to highlight the notion that all division relies on place-value understanding. The cameras allowed students across the spectrum to contribute to the final product and to focus in on the manipulation of the base-ten materials. We were trying to appeal to the visual-spatial learners in the group and to provide for them a physical model for the mental process that capable mathematicians use when doing mental division.

Student Exploration of the Problem

Students fell to the task quickly. They established how many blocks they needed to start with and who would be "on" with the camera first. As we wandered around the room, we prompted for mathematical language. "What is the dividend? How did you build it?" We encouraged students to use this specific language in their recordings.

Trading for tens was a fairly evident next step, but then when students were left with 75 blocks (7 tens and 5 singles) to share among the 15 groups, many stopped and talked with their peers to establish what to do next. "You can share out the tens evenly. You have to break them all up into singles first. Make an exchange. That'll be 75 singles." We teachers met at the back of the room and celebrated the place-value language being used.

Establishing Criteria and Problem Solving

The classroom was noisy and busy — cameras flashed and materials were being assembled and disassembled. We stopped the students midway through the task for a "commercial break" and held up some student work. "I notice that this group is including key words in their work," I said. "Listen to this statement — it is clear what happened in this step."

Our thinking in having students use the digital camera was to force them to stop and record each stage as it was performed, and to be mindful of the process they were following.

Students with more verbal-linguistic capacity helped those who struggled to write and record the step when it was their turn.

Modeling students' use of language helps to spark other children's thinking and clarify the expectation midway through the task.

We invited another group to share the problem they were having with their solution. There were 15 groups of 24 blocks and 9 leftover blocks to one side.

"I think we lost some," Rachel mused. "There's not enough to go around." The other members of her group looked befuddled. They knew that there had to be an equal number in each group because the question said so.

We asked: "Is there a way you could figure out how many you have? Does anyone have a suggestion for Rachel and her group?"

Someone pulled out a calculator and wandered over to help. We ended the break and students began working again. Rachel and Sean, a member of the same group, sorted out how many cubes they had by multiplying 15 × 24 and adding the 9 leftover single blocks.

"We only have 369 blocks," Rachel said, then counted on her fingers. "We need 1, 2, 3, 4, 5, 6 more." This kind of error analysis and self-correction told us a lot about Rachel and Sean's thinking about division and its relationship to multiplication.

Step 1: We made the dividend with 3 blocks of 100, 7 blocks of 10, and 5 singles.

Step 2: We broke up the hundreds into tens. We had 30 tens, 7 tens from before, and 5 singles.

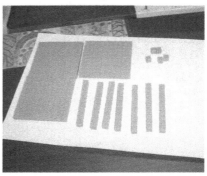

Step 3: We put the 30 tens into 15 sets.

Step 4: We turned the 7 tens that were left over into singles. We took the 75 singles and put them into 15 groups of 4.

Step 5: We realized we could add 1 more single to each group of 4 and did so.

Step 6: We made 15 groups of 25, with 2 tens and 5 ones in each group.

After: Personalizing and Transforming

Strategy Sharing and Consolidation

As the class drew to a close, students had a chance to share their solutions, their strategies for solving the problem, and any difficulties that had come up for them. Some made connections to the problem Rachel's group had with lost pieces and talked about how they figured out how many pieces should be in each set of collector cards. We talked about the method they had used to find the quotient, and how in each case it involved breaking up hundreds, tens, and singles. We took one group's collaborative work and read it, then modeled a way to record their thinking.

Explicitly saying and recording your thinking for the students helps develop deeper understanding of the process and move beyond memorizing algorithms.

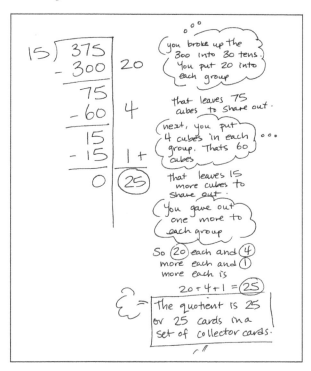

The method shown is one featured in many newer math programs and is a far more sensible algorithm for representing and communicating the act of dividing. As a process, it relies on meaning and is whole-number based rather than digit based as traditional long division is.

"You started with a dividend of 375 and a divisor of 15. Let's write that down . . ." We demonstrated the way students normally structure a traditional long-division algorithm, but made connections to the actual movement of the materials and the place-value work the students had done. Making the connection between how to solve it and how to represent it is critical for students.

To conclude the lesson, we summarized what we had learned and set the stage for them to use their new knowledge:

> There are lots of ways to divide — using mental division, using base-ten materials to model the problem, using the repeated subtraction method for representing the process. All of these methods depend on place value — how we use ones, tens, and hundreds. Next week we'll have the chance to practise these and more strategies for division.

Reflecting and Practice

The next day, Liz asked her students to write about the task. One ELL student responded as follows:

> The troubles I had is that I could easily do the operation in my head, but it was hard for me to put into words and steps because I didn't remember doing math division that kind of way so it was neat to me. Another trouble I had was that I was confused with the steps because for example 30 divided by 5. I build the number and broke the 100 into tens, and 3 tens into 30 ones. Then it was confusing because I did not know if you put that 2 broke up tables into steps or ones. But the rest I thought was easily to understand.

As practice and consolidation, students were asked to use any method they wanted to in solving a range of division problems — some involving remainders, some without.

It is important to recognize that the volume of practice was not what we were used to. Six questions were assigned to students in each grade level in this combined-grade classroom (Grade 6 students worked on the same concept but with thousands rather than hundreds).

- Initially, only three questions were presented.
- Two additional questions were word problems requiring students to read and determine the dividend and divisor in each case before solving the problem.
- The final question was a more open-ended and complex one: students were given a quotient, for example, "13 R 6." They were asked to explain what the dividend and divisor might be in each case, and then to explain their thinking. This "reverse procedure" question provided challenge for learners at the upper end of the spectrum because they were encouraged to explain how they had chosen their dividend and divisor, and what patterns they could see when comparing multiple solutions. Likewise, the question was accessible to other students who could build and visualize a simpler solution — and still achieve the learning goals for the lesson.

Through their practice answering these questions, students gained ownership of the math skills.

The Making of Mathematicians

Liz and I talked after the lesson. We commented on the time we took with our in-class math explorations, and our initial worry about assigning fewer practice problems. Then, however, we reflected on the students' increased understanding of the content and of their ability to communicate their thinking. This is the making of mathematicians.

Conclusion: Making a Difference for All

Our classrooms are richer, more vibrant learning spaces when all students are included. Although a diverse group of students may pose more challenges to us as teachers, overcoming these challenges is within our reach. As teachers, we plan with the class in mind and build in supports, as necessary, for individual students or small groups of students. We believe that our students have more, not less, in common with each other. We believe that they want to be with us and their classroom community and that they all want to belong. In order to belong, they must be involved in the academic curriculum as well as in the social curriculum. We are challenged to know each of our students and to figure out how we can provide entry points into the curriculum so that each student is appropriately challenged and engaged in learning. Doing so requires knowing what our students can do, knowing what our students need to be able to do, choosing a focus for learning, designing a plan to achieve this focus, and being explicit with our learning goals.

- **Collaborating**

Collaboration is key. Being a member of a learning team — perhaps composed of a learning resource teacher, a librarian, an administrator, and classroom teachers — is the first step in refining our professional practice. In our experience, having the opportunity to work side by side with another teacher in the classroom, for even a small amount of time, enriches our teaching and benefits all students. Students with special needs — identified or not — thrive when their learning goals are embedded in the classroom curriculum. Working collaboratively with learning resource teachers helps us to develop supports and strategies that benefit all students. We learn from observing the practice and interactions of another professional, even while teaching ourselves. When not working within the classroom, we prize co-planning lessons and units. The powerful conversations that occur in co-planning, co-reflecting, and co-analyzing student work energize us and propel us on to new learning.

- **Using Data to Inform Instruction**

Assessment has taken on new meanings for us. We have shifted more and more from an emphasis on using data for reporting out progress, to using data to inform our instruction and our students' learning. This shift has helped us become more explicit in designing our teaching lessons, which has, in turn, caused a more profound growth in our students' learning. Our students are developing their capacity as self-regulating learners. To promote this, we work to include our students in our assessment conversations, since they are the most in need of the information. They are learning to ask: *"What do I need to be able to do? What can I do now? What support will I need to learn? How will I know when I have achieved this goal?"* This stance is a critical one for them to take, as these questions fuel self-regulated learning.

- **Helping Students Feel Safe and Engaged**

To learn well, students need to feel emotionally safe and to be actively engaged. In planning our lesson sequences and our big idea–based units, we keep in mind the need to be constantly building strong classroom communities where all students do feel safe and can take risks in their learning. We "walk the talk," prizing differences and demonstrating how much more we learn through these differences. We are also keenly aware of the importance of engagement. To this end, we employ strategies that will invite different modes and preferences for learning — working with words, with drawing, with models, inside and outside the classroom — inviting students into activity. Most important, we value and welcome their background knowledge. We build from what they know and the social and cultural funds of knowledge that they bring.

- **Offering Voice and Choice**

Over the years, we have witnessed the loss of voice and choice for students yet voice and choice are critical elements for inviting learners into learning. Voice and choice are the foundation of classroom structures such as Writers Workshop and literature circles. They are celebrated in strategies such as Quadrants of a Thought and dialogue journals. They are possible in daily tasks where criteria have been established for the product or performance, and where a variety of ways are presented to display learning. Everyone can be collectively involved in learning without everyone doing exactly the same thing. This stance is what ensures that all students are learning to the best of their abilities.

- **Making Connections**

Deep learning — learning that stays with us and is mulled around in our minds — grows as a result of connections. Through all that we do, we thread the theme of making connections. We use personal connections to introduce a new theme or unit; personal and text connections to make sense of and process new information; and personal, text, and world connections to transform and personalize new understandings. We also use the same thread of connections to help students build personal repertoires of learning strategies, ways of thinking and learning that they can use without any dependence on us.

- **Taking Time**

All of this takes time. To profoundly affect student learning requires deep, thoughtful conversation and activity, involvement, and time. We are in a rush to be the best teachers we can be, but are not to hurry students through a curriculum without their becoming lifelong, passionate, inquisitive learners.

Finally, we believe that there is no one right way. We have presented a sampling of exemplary classroom practices from diverse classrooms where all students are learning. We present these to you as models, but not as one right answer. Your best results will occur when you do as we have done: learn with each other, ask about one another's approaches, keep an active mental model of learning, and draw on your experiences, professional learning community, reflections, and *students* to move you on to new possibilities.

Bibliography

Allington, Richard. 2004. Lower Mainland Council of the International Reading Association (LOMCIRA) Fall Conference, Vancouver, BC.

Allington, Richard, and Peter Johnston. 2001. "Characteristics of Exemplary Fourth Grade Instruction." In *Learning to Teach Reading: Setting the Research Agenda*, edited by Cathy M. Roller. Newark, DE: International Reading Association.

Atwell, Nancie. 1998. *In the Middle: New Understandings about Writing, Reading, and Learning*, 2nd ed. Portsmouth, NH: Heinemann.

———. 2002. *Lessons That Change Writers.* Portsmouth, NH: Heinemann.

Beers, Kylene. 2002. *When Kids Can't Read — What Teachers Can Do.* Portsmouth, NH: Heinemann.

Biancarosa, Gina, and Catherine E. Snow. 2004. *Reading Next: A Vision for Action and Research in Middle and High School Literacy: A Report to Carnegie Corporation of New York.* Washington, DC: Alliance for Excellent Education.

British Columbia Ministry of Education and Ministry Responsible for Multiculturalism and Human Rights. 1994. *Evaluating Reading across Curriculum: Using the Reading Reference Set to Support Learning and Enhance Communication.* Victoria, BC: BC Ministry of Education.

British Columbia Ministry of Education. 2009. *BC Performance Standards: Reading.* Victoria, BC: British Columbia Ministry of Education, Student Assessment and Program Evaluation Branch.

Brownlie, Faye. 2004. *Literacy in the Middle Years: Part 1*, webcast. www.bced. gov.bc.ca/literacy/webcast.htm.

———. 2005. *Literacy in the Middle Years: Part 2*, webcast. www.bced.gov.bc.ca/ literacy/webcast.htm.

———. 2005. *Grand Conversations, Thoughtful Responses.* Winnipeg, MB: Portage & Main Press.

Brownlie, Faye, Susan Close, and Linda Wingren. 1988. *Reaching for Higher Thought.* Edmonton, AB: Arnold.

Brownlie, Faye, Catherine Feniak, and Vicki McCarthy. 2004. *Instruction and Assessment of ESL Learners: Promoting Success in Your Classroom.* Winnipeg, MB: Portage & Main Press.

Brownlie, Faye, Carole Fullerton, and Leyton Schnellert. 2011. *It's All about Thinking: Collaborating to Support All Learners in Mathematics and Science.* Winnipeg, MB: Portage & Main Press.

Brownlie, Faye, and Judith King. 2011. *Learning in Safe Schools*, 2nd ed. Markham, ON: Pembroke.

Brownlie, Faye, and Leyton Schnellert. 2009. *It's All about Thinking: Collaborating to Support All Learners in Humanities, Social Studies & English.* Winnipeg, MB: Portage & Main Press.

Butler, Deborah L., Leyton Schnellert, and S. C. Cartier. 2013. "Layers of Self- and Co-regulation: Teachers' Co-regulating Learning and Practice to Foster Students' Self-Regulated Learning through Reading." *Education Research International*. http://www.hindawi.com/journals/edu/2013/845694/.

Butler, Deborah L., Leyton Schnellert, and Nancy Perry. 2016. *Developing Self-Regulating Learners*. Toronto: Pearson.

Davies, Anne, Caren Cameron, Colleen Politano, and Kathleen Gregory. 1992. *Together Is Better: Collaborative Assessment, Evaluation and Reporting*. Winnipeg, MB: Peguis.

Fielding, Linda G., and P. David Pearson. 1994. "Synthesis of Research/Reading Comprehension: What Works." *Educational Leadership* 51 (5): 62–68.

Fogarty, Robin. 1990. "People Search" workshop presentation. Richmond, BC: Thoughtful Cooperative Learning Workshop.

Gardner, Howard. 1993. *Multiple Intelligences: New Horizons in Theory and Practice*. New York: Basic Books.

———. 2002. *Intelligence Reframed: Multiple Intelligences for the Twenty-First Century*. New York: Basic Books.

Graham, Steve, and Dolores Perin. 2007. *Writing Next: Effective Strategies to Improve Writing of Adolescents in Middle and High Schools — A Report to Carnegie Corporation of New York*. Washington, DC: Alliance for Excellent Education.

Graham, Steve, Alisha Bollinger, Carol Booth Olson, Catherine D'Aoust, Charles MacArthur, Deborah McCutchen, and Natalie Olinghouse. 2012. *Teaching Elementary School Students to Be Effective Writers* (NCEE 2012-4058). Washington, DC: National Center for Education Evaluation and Regional Assistance, Institute of Education Sciences, U.S. Department of Education.

Gregory, Kathleen, Caren Cameron, and Anne Davies. 2011. *Setting and Using Criteria*. Merville, BC: Connections.

Heard, Georgia. 1998. *Awakening the Heart: Exploring Poetry in Elementary and Middle School*. Portsmouth, NH: Heinemann.

Jeroski, Sharon, and Faye Brownlie. 2006. *Reading and Responding, Evaluation Resources for Teachers (Grades 4, 5, and 6)*. Scarborough, ON: Nelson Canada. [See http://www.nelsonschoolcentral.com/cgi-in/lansaweb?webapp= WAUTHOR+webrtn=author+F(LW3CONTID)=125734.]

Johnson, Pat, and Katie Keier. 2010. *Catching Readers before They Fall*. Portland, ME: Stenhouse.

Morrow, Peggy, Sharon Jeroski, Ray Appel, Carole Saundry, Cynthia Pratt Nicholson, Ken Harper, Don Dones, Michael Davis, Ralph Connelly, Nora Alexander, Jason Johnston, Bryn Keyes, Steve Thomas, Jeananne Thomas, Linda Edwards, Antonietta Lenjosek, Trevor Brown, and Maggie Martin Connell. 2006. *Math Makes Sense — Grade 6, Western Edition*. Toronto: Pearson Education Canada.

McGee, Inger. 1996. "Grand Conversations as Social Contexts for Literary Work." Paper presented at the American Education Research Association Conference, New York, April.

McKinsey & Company. 2007. *How the World's Best-Performing School Systems Come Out on Top*. http://mckinseyonsociety.com/how-the-worlds-best-performing-schools-come-out-on-top/

———. 2011. *How the World's Most Improved School Systems Keep Getting Better.* https://www.schoolclimate.org/climate/documents/policy/How-the-Worlds-Most-Improved-School-Systems-Keep-Getting-Better.pdf.

Pressley, Michael. 2002. "Metacognition and Self-Regulated Comprehension." In *What Research Has to Say about Reading Instruction*, edited by Alan E. Farstrup and S. Jay Samuels. Newark, DE: International Reading Association.

Ray, Katie Wood, with Lisa B. Cleaveland. 2004. *About the Authors: Writing Workshop with Our Youngest Writers.* Portsmouth, NH: Heinemann.

Reid, Janine, and Betty Schultze, with Ulla Petersen. 2012. *What's Next for This Beginning Writer?* rev. ed. Markham, ON: Pembroke.

Rose, David H., and Anne Meyer. 2002. *Teaching Every Student in the Digital Age: Universal Design for Learning.* Alexandra, VA: ASCD.

Rothstein, Vicki, and Rhoda Termansen. 1999. *Language Learning through Literature.* Austin, TX: PRO-ED.

Schnellert, Leyton, Deborah L. Butler, and Stephanie K. Higginson. 2008. "Co-constructors of Data; Co-constructors of Meaning: Teacher Professional Development in an Age of Accountability." *Teaching and Teacher Education* 24 (3): 725–75.

Schnellert, Leyton, Mehjabeen Datoo, Krista Ediger, and Joanne Panas. *Pulling Together: Integrating Inquiry, Assessment and Instruction in English Language Arts, Grades 6–12.* Markham, ON: Pembroke.

Schnellert, Leyton, Linda Watson, and Nicole Widdess. 2015. *It's All about Thinking: Creating Pathways for All Learners in the Middle Years.* Winnipeg, MB: Portage & Main Press.

Short, Kathy G. 1993. "Creating a Community of Learners." In *Talking about Books: Creating Literate Communities* by Kathy Short and Kathryn M. Pierce. Portsmouth, NH: Heinemann.

Spandel, Vicki, and Richard J. Stiggins. 1997. *Creating Writers: Linking Assessment and Instruction.* New York: Longman.

Tovani, Cris. 2004. *Do I Really Have to Teach Reading? Content Comprehension, Grades 6–12.* Portland, ME: Stenhouse.

Van de Walle, John. 2004. *Elementary and Middle School Mathematics: Teaching Developmentally.* Toronto: Pearson.

Van de Walle, John, and Lou Ann H. Lovin. 2006. *Teaching Student-Centered Mathematics: Grades 5–8.* Toronto: Pearson.

Wells, Gordon. 1986. *The Meaning Makers. Children Learning Language and Using Language to Learn.* Portsmouth, NH: Heinemann.

Wilhelm, Jeffrey D. 2013. *Improving Comprehension with Think-Aloud Strategies: Modeling What Good Readers Do.* New York: Scholastic.

Wilhelm, Jeffrey D., Tanya N. Baker, and Julie Dube. 2001. *Strategic Reading: Guiding Students to Lifelong Literacy, 6–12.* Portsmouth, NH: Heinemann.

Recommended Children's Books

Abbott, Tony. *Firegirl.* New York: Little, Brown, 2006.

Aiken, Joan. *Midnight Is a Place.* Boston: Houghton Mifflin, 2002.

Aliki. *Marianthe's Story: Painted Words, Spoken Memories.* New York: Greenwillow, 1998.

Applegate, Katherine. *Home of the Brave.* New York: Square Fish, 2008.

———. *The One and Only Ivan.* New York: HarperCollins, 2012.

Avi. *Crispin.* New York: Hyperion, 2002.

Babbitt, Natalie. *Tuck Everlasting.* New York: Farrar, Straus and Giroux, 1975.

Bell, Cece. *El Deafo.* New York: Amulet Books, 2014.

Bradby, Marie. *More Than Anything Else* [illustrated by Chris K. Soentpiet]. New York: Orchard, 1995.

Brown, Dinah. *Who Is Malala Yousafzai?* [illustrated by Andrew Thomson]. New York: Penguin Random House, 2014.

Cannon, Janell. *Stellaluna.* New York: Houghton Mifflin Harcourt, 2011.

Chang, Ying. *Revolution Is Not a Dinner Party.* New York: Henry Holt, 2008.

Cherry, Lynne. *The River Ran Wild.* New York: Harcourt Brace Jovanovich, 1992.

Chikwanine, Michel, and Jessica Dee Humphreys. *Child Soldier: When Boys and Girls Are Used in War* [illustrated by Claudia Dávila]. Toronto: Kids Can Press, 2015.

Cole, Henry. *Unspoken: A Story from the Underground Railroad.* New York: Scholastic, 2012.

Collier, James, and Christopher Collier. *Jump Ship to Freedom.* New York: Dell, 1987.

Cooper, Floyd. *Juneteenth for Mazie.* North Mankato, MN: Capstone, 2015.

Cutler, Jane. *The Cello of Mr. O.* New York: Dutton Children's Books, 1999.

D'Adamo, Francesco. *Iqbal.* New York: Atheneum/Simon and Shuster, 2003.

Dickens, Charles. *Oliver Twist.* New York: Tor Classics, 1994.

Doherty, Berlie. *Street Child.* London: Collins, 1995.

Draper, Sharon M. *Copper Sun.* New York: Harper, 2008.

———. *Out of My Mind.* New York: Atheneum Books for Young Readers, 2010.

Duncan Edwards, Pamela. *Barefoot.* New York: HarperCollins, 1998.

Ellis, Deborah. *The Breadwinner.* Toronto: Groundwood, 2001 [first in a trilogy including *Parvana's Journey* and *Mud City*].

———. *Parvana's Journey.* Toronto: Groundwood, 2003.

———. *The Heaven Shop.* Markham, ON: Fitzhenry & Whiteside, 2004.

———. *Mud City.* Toronto: Groundwood, 2004.

Fleischman, Paul. *Weslandia.* Somerville, MA: Candlewick Paperbacks, 2002.

Frank, Anne. *The Diary of Anne Frank.* New York: Simon and Schuster, 1952.

Fullerton, Alma. *Libertad.* Markham, ON: Fitzhenry & Whiteside, 2008.

Greenberg, Polly. *O Lord, I Wish I Was a Buzzard*. New York: Seastar Books, 2002.

Haddix, Margaret Peterson. *Among the Hidden* (Shadow Children #1). New York: Aladdin, 2000.

Hamilton, Virginia. *The People Could Fly*. New York: Knopf, 2007.

Haskins, Jim. *Get on Board: The Story of the Underground Railroad*. New York: Scholastic, 1997.

Heide, Florence Parry, and Judith Heide Gilliland. *Sami and the Time of the Troubles*. New York: Clarion, 1992.

Heneghan, James. *The Grave*. Toronto: Groundwood Books/Douglas & McIntyre, 2000.

Ho, Minfong. *The Clay Marble*. New York: Farrar, Straus and Giroux, 2003.

Jamieson, Victoria. *Roller Girl*. New York: Dial Books for Young Readers, 2015.

Jordan-Fenton, Christy. *Fatty Legs: A True Story*. Toronto: Annick, 2010.

Kaplan, William, and Shelley Tanaka. *One More Border: The True Story of One Family's Escape from War-Torn Europe*. Vancouver: Douglas & McIntyre, 1998.

Kidd, Diana. *Onion Tears*. New York: Harper Trophy, 1993.

Kogawa, Joy. "Hiroshima Exit." In *Themes on the Journey*, edited by Barry James. Scarborough, ON: Nelson, 1989.

Kositsky, Lynne. *A Mighty Big Imagining*. Toronto: Penguin, 2001.

———. *Rachael: The Maybe House*. Toronto: Penguin, 2003.

Lai, Thanhha. *Inside Out and Back Again*. New York: HarperCollins, 2011.

Laird, Elizabeth. *Kiss the Dust*. London: Mammoth, 1991.

———. *Secret Friends*. London: Hodder Children's Books, 1996.

———. *The Garbage King*. London: Macmillan Children's Books, 2003.

———. *Oranges in No Man's Land*. London: Macmillan Children's Books, 2016.

Lang, Suzanne, and Max Lang. *Families, Families, Families!* New York: Random House Children's Books, 2015.

LeBox, Annette. *Salmon Creek*. Toronto: Groundwood, 2002.

Lester, Julius. *Day of Tears*. New York: Hyperion, 2007.

Levine, Ellen. *Henry's Freedom Box: A True Story from the Underground Railroad*. New York: Scholastic, 2007.

Lord, Cynthia. *Rules*. New York: Scholastic, 2006.

Lowry, Lois. *Number the Stars*. New York: Bantam, 1989.

Lyons, Mary E. *Letters from a Slave Girl*. New York: Scribner, 1992.

Martin, Ann M. *Belle Teal*. New York: Scholastic, 2005.

McCoola, Marika. *Baba Yaga's Assistant* [illustrated by Emily Carroll]. Somerville, MA: Candlewick Press, 2015.

Mikaelsen, Ben. *Touching Spirit Bear*. New York: HarperCollins, 2001.

Moore, Cathy. *Ellen Craft's Escape from Slavery*. Minneapolis, MN: Lerner, 2010.

Mulligan, Andy. *Trash*. Oxford, UK: David Fickling Books, 2010.

Myers, Walter Dean. *The Glory Field*. New York: Scholastic, 2008.

Naidoo, Beverley. *Journey to Jo'burg*. New York: Harper Trophy, 1988.

———. *No Turning Back*. New York: Harper Trophy, 1999.

Nielsen, Susin. *Word Nerd*. Toronto: Tundra, 2008.

———. *The Reluctant Journey of Henry K. Larsen*. Toronto: Tundra, 2012.

———. *We Are All Made of Molecules*. Toronto: Tundra, 2015.

Nye, Naomi Shihab. *Habibi*. New York: Simon Pulse, 1999.

Palacio, R. J. *Wonder*. New York: Knopf, 2012.

Park, Linda Sue. *A Single Shard*. New York: Yearling, 2001.

Paterson, Katherine. *Jip: His Story*. New York: Penguin, 1998.

Paulson, Gary. *Sarny: A Life Remembered*. New York: Delacorte Press, 1997.

Polacco, Patricia. *January's Sparrow*. New York: Philomel Books, 2009.

Ringgold, Faith. *Aunt Harriet's Underground Railroad in the Sky*. New York: Crown, 1992.

Robertson, David. *7 Generations: A Plains Cree Saga* [illustrated by Scott B. Henderson]. Winnipeg, MB: HighWater Press, 2013.

Rotner, Shelly, and Sheila M. Kelly. *Families*. New York: Holiday House, 2015.

Shaskan, Stephen. *A Dog Is a Dog*. San Francisco: Chronicle Books, 2011.

Shea, Pegi Deitz. *The Carpet Boy's Gift* [illustrated by Leane Morin]. Gardiner, ME: Tilbury House, 2006.

Sterling, Dorothy. *Freedom Train: The Story of Harriet Tubman*. Toronto: Scholastic, 1954.

Sterling, Shirley. *My Name Is Seepeetza*. Vancouver: Douglas & McIntyre, 1992.

Stroud, Bettye. *The Patchwork Path: A Quilt Map to Freedom*. Somerville, MA: Candlewick, 2007.

Tan, Shaun. *Tales from Outer Suburbia*. New York: Arthur Levine, 2008.

Tarshis, Lauren. *I Survived the Attacks of September 11, 2001* [illustrated by Scott Dawson]. New York: Scholastic, 2012.

Van Draanen, Wendelin. *The Running Dream*. New York: Knopf, 2011.

Velchin, Eugene. *Breaking Stalin's Nose*. New York: Henry Holt, 2011.

Walters, Eric. *Sketches*. Toronto: Penguin, Canada, 2007.

———. *Walking Home*. Toronto: Doubleday Canada, 2014.

Waterton, Betty, and Ann Blades. *A Salmon for Simon*. Vancouver: Douglas & McIntyre, 2013.

Whelan, Gloria. *Goodbye, Vietnam*. New York: Random House, 1992.

Williams, Laura. *Behind the Bedroom Wall*. Minneapolis, MN: Milkweed, 1996.

Wilson, Janet. *Our Rights: How Kids Are Changing the World*. Toronto: Second Story Press, 2013.

Winters, Jeanette. *Follow the Drinking Gourd*. New York: Knopf, 1992.

Woodson, Jacqueline. *Show Way*. New York: Putnam, 2005.

Wright, Betty Ren. *The Ghost of Popcorn Hill*. New York: Scholastic, 1994.

Yousafzai, Malala, with Christina Lamb. *My Name Is Malala: The Girl Who Stood Up for Education and Was Shot by the Taliban*. Boston: Little, Brown, 2013.

Zhang, Ange. *Red Land, Yellow River: A Story from the Cultural Revolution*. Vancouver: Douglas & McIntyre, 2004.

Index